**Development
Reconsidered**

Development Reconsidered

Bridging the Gap Between Government and People

Edgar Owens
and
Robert Shaw

Lexington Books

D.C. Heath and Company
Lexington, Massachusetts
Toronto　　　London

Third printing with changes August 1974

Published simultaneously in Canada.

Printed in the United States of America.

International Standard Book Number: 0-669-81729-5

Library of Congress Catalog Card Number: 79-184297

Table of Contents

List of Figures

List of Tables

Foreword to Third Printing

In the original Foreword Bradford Morse, then a Member of the House Foreign Affairs Committee and now Undersecretary General of the United Nations, and I wrote, "It is time for a serious re-evaluation by Congress and the American people of what the United States should do about foreign aid." The Congress began such a re-evaluation May 30, 1973 when twenty-five of my colleagues and I on the House Committee introduced a series of amendments designed to incorporate into U.S. foreign aid policy a participation strategy for which *Development Reconsidered* is the intellectual backdrop. Other foreign aid agencies, among them the World Bank, are reviewing the same issues that our Congress has now acted upon.

When the bill was signed into law by the President on December 17, 1973 the United States became the first of the rich countries to shift away from "trickle-down" to people-oriented development. Redirecting our efforts toward the poor who make up the overwhelming majority of people in the developing countries conforms to the instinctive concern of Americans that past foreign aid programs have not reached the people we have wanted to help.

Donald M. Fraser
House Foreign Affairs Committee

Foreword

This book would only be more timely if we could have had the benefit of its insights during the 1971 foreign assistance debate. For the first time in its legislative history, the foreign aid program was defeated by the Senate. It survived a hurried and, in many ways, unsatisfactory last-minute Senate-House compromise.

While foreign aid has often been controversial in this country, Americans generally have supported the program—not only because it seemed right for such a rich country to share its wealth, but also because it seemed a wise investment in the future. Money and Western knowhow were intended to help bridge the gap between the industrialized countries and the developing nations.

However, there has been a growing realization in the United States—expressed in the Senate vote—that we are not achieving what we set out to accomplish through foreign aid to the developing countries. Expectant hopes are not being fulfilled. While development is progressing well in a few countries, poverty and unemployment, illiteracy and disease are still endemic throughout the developing world. Political and social problems abound everywhere.

What has gone wrong?

Development has turned out to be a much more complicated problem than had been thought when the foreign aid program began. In the beginning, it was assumed the solution lay in merely transplanting the same kind of techniques and knowhow that have been the key to progress for most of the Western world, accompanied by enough money to allow these vital techniques to take root in their new environment. But the transplants haven't worked.

Then, too, *realpolitik* has more often than not governed our relationships with the less developed world. Foreign aid has been used as an adjunct to our Cold War efforts in Africa, Asia and Latin America. But the enduring friendship of governments or people does not depend on guns or money or even technical expertise. Nor do they win the allegiance of a people to their own government. Sometimes our efforts to win the support of a government for international political reasons have turned its people against us. As our foreign aid programs have become identified with elitist governments and programs that favor the rich, they only widen the gap and deepen the discontent with the people we want most to help.

Similarly, within the United States, a once honorable aid program has fallen into disrepect. Even members of Congress who usually support aid programs have been voicing their doubts about the U.S. foreign aid program—ourselves among them. On a number of occasions, some members of Congress have tried to reduce military aid and increase economic aid so that our aid programs would reach their intended beneficiaries—the people living in poverty and despair in the developing countries. Yet, the foreign aid policy of 1972 is not much changed from a decade ago.

That the accumulated frustrations of years should have erupted into public debate about the future of foreign aid should not have been unexpected. Indeed, in retrospect, the Senate action is not nearly as surprising as it seemed the day the vote was taken. Why should Congress vote to continue a program which has created so much disillusionment both at home and abroad? If foreign aid is to be continued, a meaningful aid policy must be developed and articulated—a policy that the American people can believe in once more, a policy which the people in developing countries can respect.

If we have learned nothing else about the development process, we have learned that development cannot be exported. It is a process of change that must be sustained by the government and the people within each country, a process that should work to the benefit of all. The central problem of development is to find out how this dynamic process of change can be set in motion within each country. As Edgar Owens points out, the real issue to consider in discussing U.S. participation in development, is not "foreign aid" but development itself! What is fundamentally involved is the kind of relationship that should exist between the United States and the developing countries. These are the themes of *Development Reconsidered*. It is a long-overdue discussion of development oriented to increasing benefits for the people, rather than increasing the gross national product as a statistical measure. Its suggestions are provocative and controversial. But they emerge from a necessary insistence that we must change the basic framework in which we think and talk about development if we are ever to break away from the unproductive programs of the past. It is time for a serious reevaluation by Congress and the American people of what the United States should do about foreign aid.

Bradford Morse
Under Secretary General, United Nations

Donald Fraser
House Foreign Affairs Committee

Preface

Winston Churchill, like the Bible and Shakespeare, seems to have a quotation for every purpose. "Writing a book is an adventure. To begin with, it is a joy and an amusement. Then it becomes a mistress. And then it becomes a master. Then it becomes a tyrant, and in the last phase, when you are reconciled to your servitude, you kill the monster."

My search for a humane strategy of development began seven years ago when I was a Federal Executive Fellow of the Brookings Institution, Washington, D.C. Mostly I learned that the conventional approach to "economic development" did not fit very well with my personal experiences with Asian villagers.

The search for an answer to a question as complex as development is, of course, never ending. To write a book in such a circumstance is to stop at a moment in time to consider whether common threads in human experience can be converted into principles that might give people a better chance of achieving their purpose—in this instance, success in development.

This book is based on my conviction that principles of development are universal; that after two decades of development and foreign aid a number of these principles can be identified and used to explain how a handful of countries have organized relatively successful development programs; and that other poor countries can improve their development performance—if governments possess the political will. In discussing these principles one need always remember that the principles can be useful guides to development policy only if they are applied with enormous flexibility and imagination in the great diversity of countries and cultures in the Third World.

This book was begun as several papers, now incorporated into Chapters 2, 4 and 5, for a seminar conducted by the Southeast Asia Development Advisory Group in February 1971. Pressed for time while still working, I asked Robert Shaw, a brilliant young English student of development, to help me expand these papers into a full-length manuscript. Mr. Shaw was Administrator of the British Volunteer Program in Tanzania, 1966-1968. Since then he has been studying at Princeton University and working with the Overseas Development Council in Washington. He has already become a recognized authority on the employment problem in the poor countries. Mr. Shaw was especially helpful in writing the first four chapters and the last.

In a different sense, however, this book took shape in conversations with villagers and the urban poor in a number of Asian countries where I have worked or traveled as an official of the United States Agency for International Development. What these marginal people have taught me is this: if we Westerners are to be able to help solve the problem of development we cannot think as we do at home. We must, instead, learn how to think like the illiterate and hungry in the villages and shanty towns of the Third World.

So many people have helped me through the years, wherever I have been living, that at times I have felt more like the secretary of a traveling seminar than an author writing in the quiet of his study. Among the many there are a few who have been exceptionally generous with their time and thought. They are Ben R. Ferguson; Linda K. Lee; Professor E.A.J. Johnson; John Eriksson, Mark Krackiewicz; Marian Stilson; Christina Schoux; Joel Darmstadter, Princeton Lyman; Cynthia Wharton; several persons in the sub-Continent whose names are perhaps better omitted during the uncertainties among India, Pakistan, and Bangladesh, which still persist as this is written; and lastly Edward B. Cooper, a fine economist with whom I first worked in Bangladesh, and whose untimely death just a few days before the manuscript was sent to the publisher was a great personal loss. For their countless improvements in both substance and style I want to express my gratitude. Whatever errors and deficiencies remain are, of course, my own responsibility.

Edgar Owens

Bethesda, Maryland
February 18, 1972

Introduction

The United States has confused its priorities and thus raised doubts as to its real foreign aid objective. Is it to help the poor countries develop, or to help achieve U.S. foreign-policy goals? The pursuit of anti-communism in the Third World is a foreign-policy goal, not a development policy that could increase yields per acre, create jobs, raise living standards, or induce people to be loyal to their government. Moreover, democracy versus communism is not the issue in villages and overcrowded shanty towns, among the illiterate and hungry. From the point of view of the poor countries, policies which will involve the people in development are a much stronger defense against potentially violent solutions than military arrangements with the United States.

The most important lesson that can be drawn from U.S.-Third World relationships during the past two decades—hopefully a lesson now learned—is that the rich countries can help the poor only if the latter possess the political will to modernize. If that will is lacking, foreign aid is not an adequate substitute. Hence, the search for an effective foreign aid policy begins in the developing countries, not in the United States.

Development Reconsidered sets forth a new strategy of development—a strategy in which participation by all the people is both the means and the end to development itself. The analysis is based more on recent historical evidence than on theory. The strategy is distilled from the relatively successful development experience of pre-war Japan, Taiwan, Korea, Egypt, Yugoslavia and, although they are commonly considered special cases, Puerto Rico and Israel. It sets forth a policy under which the great mass of small producers—farmers, artisans, "tiny" entrepreneurs—can be involved in development, in contrast to the current policy of concentrating investment in a small number of capital-intensive endeavors, mainly "modern" factories in the big cities and on large farms.

The most obvious reasons for considering a change in development policy are social and economic. Such a change would 1) enable small producers to increase their incomes through their own efforts, and 2) create enough jobs to employ the exploding labor force. Development based on a combination of participation and a labor-intensive rather than machine-intensive pattern of investment reduces the cost of increasing GNP per dollar. Such a change in the investment pattern would 3) maximize economic efficiency. A policy which is more equitable and can reduce poverty and accelerate the creation of new jobs actually represents a more efficient use of economic resources than the current pattern of investment in the Third World mentioned above, which tends to widen the gap between rich and poor.

The current pattern of investment is based on the assumption that development today in Asia, Latin America, and Africa would be essentially a repetition of development in the nineteenth century West. By now it is clear that we need to employ great caution in using Western history as a guide in formulating developing policies today, as the following illustrates. It has been a premise of Western economics that savings rates in the lower income groups are low because people on limited incomes spend their money first on consumer goods and services. Hence, government policies designed to increase savings and investment are aimed chiefly at the higher income groups. When the lower income groups are paid in wages and salaries—factory and white-collar workers—the premise holds true, in Japan as well as in Europe and North America. If these people do not own farms or businesses, they spend their money on consumer items.

Suppose, however, that the lower income groups can increase their incomes by investing in economic facilities which they own (or control through "modern" contractual arrangements). Would they still spend their money on consumer goods and services? or would they save and invest?

From the history of recently successful countries and the little research that has been done on this point, it now appears that the savings rates of lower income groups can be very high—if they own (or rent) their own economic facilities, and if governments create a nationwide network of financial institutions and economic incentives.[a]

Considerable political mischief can be caused by such mechanical transfers of Western premises. To continue the above example, the tradition of the few ruling the many has been justified, however unwittingly, by Western economists. The deeply rooted belief of many educated officials in developing countries that the poor are incapable of improving themselves and must have their decisions made for them, has been reinforced by the Western notion that, in any case, poor people are unable to save enough to pay the costs of their own improvement. Hence, it is argued, development programs that benefit the poor may well slow down economic growth because money that ought to be used for "productive investment" is used instead to subsidize the poor. Since Westerners are partly the cause of this kind of mischief, it is now incumbent upon us to be more careful in applying our experience to the very different circumstances of the developing countries.

. A word is needed about the countries cited in this book as examples of relatively successful development. Sometimes the "successful" countries are said to be special cases. For that reason, it is argued, their experience is said to be nontransferable to other developing countries. For example, Taiwan's success is attributed to the large amount of foreign aid provided by the United States—about $150 per person between 1950 and 1965. However large this amount may seem, it is small compared to the export earnings of the oil- and mineral-rich

---

[a]In a recent study of a number of lower income groups in Japan it was found that among those paid in wages and salaries, debts (for home mortgages, consumer durables, education, and such) often exceeded savings. In very sharp contrast, groups in the same income brackets who owned (or rented) economic facilities saved and invested as much as 20 to 30 percent of their incomes, a very high rate. Keith Marsden, "Towards a Synthesis of Economic Growth and Social Justice," *International Labor Review* Vol. 100, No. 5 (November 1969): 412-414.

countries. Venezuela, for example, earns $150 per person from petroleum exports in only 7 months, Chile from mineral exports in just 18 months. If money were the catalyst of development, then the oil- and mineral-rich countries ought to have the best development performance in the world. Yet these countries have not succeeded in solving some of the more crucial problems of development, such as getting agriculture moving or creating enough jobs to employ their exploding labor forces.

I do not believe the impressive record of local government in Yugoslavia, industrial decentralization in Israel, farmer cooperatives in Egypt, or the integration of industrial and agricultural development in Taiwan can be explained solely by the large amounts of foreign aid received from the United States or Russia. I do believe that when the governments of the poor countries combine participation in development with reasonable policies, then foreign aid can help the countries escape from poverty.

In discussions of United States participation in development, the issue to consider is not foreign aid, but development itself. Policies that will enable the developing countries to reduce poverty, increase employment and lessen inequities are the same policies that the aid agencies should support, be they bilateral—such as the U.S. Agency for International Development—or multi-national—such as the World Bank. For this reason, the first eight chapters of this book pertain to development. In the last chapter we shall examine what is commonly and too narrowly called foreign aid. What is really involved is the kind of relationship that should exist between the rich countries and the poor.

1 Development Reconsidered

The poor man's conscience is clear; yet he is ashamed. . . . He feels himself out of sight of the others, groping in the dark. Mankind takes no notice of him. He rambles and wanders unheeded. . . . In the midst of a crowd, at church, in the market . . . he is in as much obscurity as he could be in a garret or cellar. He is not disapproved, censured, or reproached; he is only not seen. To be wholly overlooked, and to know it, is intolerable.[1]

John Adams

Why should the people of the United States support foreign aid? Our country spends very little for this purpose—less than 1/2 of 1 percent of our national income and less than 2 percent of the federal budget. Yet this question is raised increasingly as we grapple with domestic priorities and desire to avoid any future Vietnam-type war.

To understand the present crisis of confidence, we should perhaps look back twenty-five years to the beginning of foreign aid—the Marshall Plan. This plan to rehabilitate Europe had both a wellspring and an objective. The wellspring was the generosity of a people expressing their desire to help other nations in need. The objective was to build a Europe in which democracy would flourish and which consequently would be strong enough to resist communism. If "World" is read for "Europe," these two elements became the rationale for the foreign aid program to the poor countries of the world during the 1950s and 60s.

Today, two decades into the Age of Development, we face an unprecedented wave of disillusionment with foreign aid. In the beginning we had high hopes for the future of both democracy and economic growth in the poor countries. Yet, only one nation and a commonwealth have become both democratic and developed—Israel and Puerto Rico—and neither is a typical developing country. Elsewhere in the Third World there are only a few countries in which the lot of the poor is being improved.

In historical terms, the economic growth rate in the Third World has been high. The 5 percent annual increase in gross national product achieved as a Third World average during the 1960s, and, which was the quantitative target for the United Nations' First Development Decade, is roughly double the rate of economic growth achieved in ninteenth-century Western Europe and North America.

Yet, in spite of this impressive overall rate of growth, the great mass of people in the poor countries remain appallingly poor and little involved in development.

1

In rural India some 150 million people still exist on less than subsistence income, and that income is estimated to be only $50 per year. Perhaps 200 million others live only a little above the level of subsistence.[2]

In Colombia, it is thought that about a third of the urban population is living at or below the level of subsistence. Sixty-five percent of the farmers cultivate only 5 percent of the farm land. The poorest third of the peasants in Colombia (and probably many other countries as well) may be no better off than when the Age of Development began. Meanwhile, 0.2 percent of the shareholders (themselves a very small group) own 61 percent of all industrial shares.[3] Income and wealth are highly concentrated in the hands of a small elite.

In many cities of the Third World, unemployment rates are as high as 15 to 20 percent and are rising, not falling![4] Yet, at the same time, migrants are pouring into the cities from the rural areas, creating vast problems of unemployment, slums, crime, and disease. These examples provide vivid refutation of the idea that global poverty is being alleviated. And the frequency of both successful and unsuccessful attacks upon governments confutes the idea that the countries are learning how to combine change with relative social stability.

This expansion of poverty at the same time the countries are getting richer in GNP has created a nagging sense among the people of the United States that our humanitarian impulse has been misdirected. Not only has foreign aid appeared to be a way of involving and then entangling our country in situations that deteriorate into violence, but foreign aid dollars have also often seemed to increase the gap between rich and poor. Somehow our assistance does not seem to have reached the heart of the problem—unemployment, the exploding population, the growing wretchedness of the urban slums, illiteracy, malnutrition, and disease. And if our foreign aid is strengthening policies that are destabilizing, then much of the criticism is justified.

Yet, most of our people realize that in the long run the condition of the developing countries will have a profound effect on the environment, our international relations, our prospects for investment, for trade and travel, and above all, perhaps, the moral climate of our society and the world.

These concerns highlight the question of what future lies in store for the poor countries of the world. And we must ask: Can the United States help eradicate the poverty that pervades these countries? These are the central issues to be examined in this book. We believe that the future of the world, from the points of view of stability and morality, is unlikely to be healthy if existing trends in the poor countries continue. We believe also that there are the beginnings of alternative approaches, approaches which can combine economic growth with social justice and greater participation by the individual in his society. Furthermore, we think the United States can play a role—both in helping to develop these approaches and in assisting their implementation—assuming that the governments in the poor countries want their peoples to become involved in development.

At the heart of these new approaches is the concept of broad-based development. By this we mean the establishment of a set of institutions which would give the underprivileged person in the poor countries an opportunity to participate in the decisions most important to his life and which, furthermore, would link him to the mainstream of modern society. By mobilizing local energies in this way, the poor can be encouraged to invest more in their own futures, to raise their incomes through higher production, and to have a greater say in the distribution of that production. Development thus can become a process in which all the people in the poor countries participate as opposed to merely the elites who are at present monopolizing the economic, social, and political benefits of development.

Frequently, this concept of broad-based development has appeared in the rhetoric of national leaders. But its implementation has been feeble because governments have been unable or unwilling to search for answers to some fundamental questions. Among the most important of these questions are: How can governments grant measures of local autonomy without splintering the fragile nation-state? How can savings be generated if income is to be distributed equitably? How can the need for rapidly rising GNP be reconciled with the need to create jobs for the exploding labor force.

In our view these dichotomies, though widely believed, are false. Creating a viable nation-state depends on galvanizing local energies; a high savings rate depends on giving the mass of people in the country the incentive and opportunity to save; and faster economic growth depends on making good use of the most abundant resources in the poor countries, particularly their workers. Yet there are only a very few countries that have tried to implement these premises. Though they are far from ideal societies, these countries have basically been much more successful than the rest of the Third World in creating the conditions of access to the mainstream of modern society for their poor. To a considerable though varying extent, these countries have applied the principles we shall discuss in this book and have thereby involved far more of their peoples in development than the great bulk of the poor countries. In this book we shall consider Taiwan, Israel, Puerto Rico, Yugoslavia, Korea, Egypt, and one program in Bangladesh (which is in suspension because of the recent political troubles). All of these countries happen to be relatively small. However, the principles of involving people in development that we shall discuss are equally relevant in large countries, such as India or Brazil, though clearly their application would be more complex because of the size and diversity of these countries.

Dual and Modernizing Societies

In examining the reasons for these differences, we shall draw a distinction throughout this book between *dual* and *modernizing* societies. This distinction

4

is, of course, only an approximation of reality: some countries fit partially into both categories. Nevertheless, we find this distinction, based on differing principles of organizing and involving people, useful in analyzing why a small number of the poor countries have been so much more successful at alleviating poverty than the rest. The basic distinction lies in the way in which these societies view the relationship between government and people. This relationship in *dual* societies is an extension of the ruler-ruled relationship of traditional societies in which decisions are essentially made at the top and passed down to the people. In *modernizing* societies there are explicit efforts to involve the populace in planning their own futures.

In dual societies the mass of ordinary people have little, if any, influence in public affairs, not even in their local communities. In John Adams' words, they live "out of sight of the others."

Dual society governments try to encourage economic growth with little trust in the capacities of their ordinary citizens. Instead, both investment and profits are concentrated in the hands of a few who are believed to have the necessary expertise and initiative. Small producers—farmers, artisans, businessmen—are not given access to the means of production, the financial system, the market, and knowledge. Village communities are essentially self-contained and are not linked upward to the much larger whole of the national society and economy. Though some information about ways of increasing production filters down to the people, there is no systematic effort to build up in local communities the knowledge base of a modern production system. These are reasons why the benefits of development still are concentrated among the few.

In order to reach the masses a dual society government does not try to organize people in their own local institutions with which central government officials can work. Rather, a dual society government tries to extend its administrative arm to the local level and to work directly with villager and townsman, to solve people's problems for them. Such a system is a way of arranging for the people to receive some of the physical paraphernalia of development—roads, schools, wells, and so on—which, in fact, are needed. However, the traditional relationship between government and people—condescension on the part of government officials and conspicuous subservience on the part of the people—remains essentially unchanged. The traditional system of rule by the few for the many, from the top down, from the center out, has simply been expanded to encompass the new goal of development. But this does not create local initiative, and even the most dedicated civil servants can only achieve a limited amount of physical change. They cannot inject changes in knowledge, attitudes and horizons for all their people through this method. As a consequence, the incomes of the mass of people do not rise, or at least not to any reasonable degree. The dual societies therefore lack that powerful engine of economic growth—the mass market. Thus, neither the social nor the economic gap between the two groups of a dual society is bridged. We can illustrate how this process functions in dual societies with the following examples:

1. The construction of such a simple project as a mile long dirt road costing only several hundred dollars requires the approval of layers of central government officials.

2. Local development projects are initiated by central government officials, not by officials of the local government, farmer cooperative, or other local organizations. When one project is completed another is not begun until and unless a central civil servant initiates the action. "These techniques produce temporary effects, but generate no sustained activity."[5] Yet development, as a matter of definition, is "sustained activity."

3. The tax powers of local governments usually are strictly limited. Land and property taxes, the traditional sources of revenue for local governments in North America and Western Europe, are commonly collected and spent by national or provincial governments. In most countries local communities are not allowed to tax themselves for their own benefit, even if they are willing.

4. Civil servants who work with local councils generally are employed, paid, promoted and transferred by the central government, a situation tantamount to having the city and county managers of the United States appointed and controlled from Washington. Not surprisingly, they feel beholden to their superiors in the national capital rather than to the people among whom they live and work.

Dual society governments have yet to learn, as did Peter the Great, that "it is difficult for a man to understand everything and to govern from a distance."[6]

It is difficult to find a situation from our own history which helps us to understand the attitude of the marginal people who live in a dual society. Perhaps the company town comes closest.

The company town, associated with such industries as mining, textiles, and logging, was organized on terms set up by the company, the equivalent of the order and control outlook of underdeveloped governments. The preferences and needs of the employees were simply ignored. If a person wanted a job he was obliged to accept the conditions of the town, not just for himself but for his family as well.

As the nineteenth century advanced, the company town came under increasing criticism. Both democratic ideas and technology were gaining rapidly. To the liberal reformers of the day the closed society of the company town was an anachronism in an increasingly open society.

As outside pressures mounted, the owners of company towns tried to satisfy their critics by sponsoring the type of activities now described as "economic development." When the reformers complained that children in the towns were not being educated, the owners built schools and hired teachers. When health conditions were deplored, the owners built dispensaries. When general physical conditions were attacked the owners improved housing, built sidewalks, paved streets and, in due time, installed electricity. And, as wages inched upward in response to competitive pressures or as the workers' share of rising productivity, the owners could claim their employees were benefiting from higher incomes as well as the company-financed improvements.

The construction projects mentioned in the preceding paragraph sometimes were built with "volunteer" labor, that is, the company provided tools and materials while the inhabitants were obliged to provide the labor force—without pay. In such a situation it would be self-deceiving for the company to assume that "volunteer" labor can be taken as evidence that the people support company policies. Yet this is the interpretation placed on "voluntary" labor in developing countries today, even though there is, in many of the countries, a tradition of unpaid (sometimes forced) labor for public works projects that can be traced back into the centuries.

Throughout the Third World during the past two decades the combination of central government donated tools and materials and "volunteer" labor by villagers has been a common method of carrying out local development projects, building such things as farm-to-market roads, wells, primary schools, especially in rural areas. In many countries, including South Vietnam, the amount of time donated for such projects by villagers has been interpreted by central government officials as a general indicator of villagers' interest in and support of government initiated development projects.

The improvements initiated by the owners of company towns satisfied neither the intended beneficiaries nor the critics. Some of the former, in fact, gradually joined in the criticism, and some of these were fired for their "anti-company behavior." In the end the company town was judged intolerable by the society in which it existed—in spite of the considerable "economic development" sponsored by the companies.

In essence the company town is an affront to the human spirit. It denies opportunity and individual expression to all but the managers, in the private lives of the people as well as on the job. By definition, it allows little individual choice, originality, creativity, and initiative. For the people there is no recourse if they want to do something different or "better" than what the company proposes.

The most that can be said for a company town is that it is benevolent. The same is true of a country governed by a small elite. Thus far, the major impact of development on the dual society governments is the addition of benevolence to the traditional functions of order and control. But benevolence is not, and never has been throughout history, a big enough idea to guide the organization of societies and governments. And in this age of competing doctrines about the organization of societies benevolence does not appear to be a big enough idea to induce loyalty.

Modernizing governments bridge the gap between traditional elites and what ought to be "the rising mass of the nation."[7] This bridge consists essentially of establishing and strengthening local institutions and systems in which the people can solve their own local problems. These local institutions and systems are then directly linked to higher levels of the economy and society so that, for example, the local cooperative is directly linked to regional and national federations of cooperatives, or, the local network of farm-to-market roads is directly linked to regional and national transportation systems.

Modernizing governments do not try to work directly with the great mass of the people. Rather, they work with the local institutions and rely upon the leaders of these institutions to work with the people. Primarily through these institutions, small producers gain access to the means of production, the financial system, the market, and knowledge for the first time. One function of these institutions is to build up in the local community the knowledge base needed to increase production. A mass market will also be gradually created because people are being drawn into the economic flow of the nation.

In a modernizing society, the relationship between government and people can evolve in the direction of mutual confidence and respect. Some measure of social stability can be achieved as people begin to feel a "sense of belonging."[8]

The difference between the attitudes of those who are governed from a distance and those who are involved in their own future is illustrated by the following two anecdotes.

As for 'development' work, in Balha, the residents of the village admit frankly that the roads and buildings, though made by them under the Community Development programme and involving a good measure of voluntary labor, are not maintained by anybody. "We make them because we are told to, and then sit back and watch in the expectation that the Block Development Officer (an official of the central government) will repair them."[9]

One old peasant told me that, when the landlord drove through the fields, he carried bodyguards on the running-boards of his car. Anyone who got in his way was shot. "Nothing could be done," the peasant replied, "since the police were in his pay." His word was law.

In 1952, the revolutionary government . . . limited land ownership to 200 acres (in 1961, reduced to 100), and the peasants joyfully distributed the pasha's land. . . . For the first time the farmers began to cultivate their own land. Production soared. Perhaps most importantly, El Westiana witnessed the birth of a sense of individual importance.

As one farmer—although unlettered and ill—put it to me: "We gained dignity and independence for the first time. I now own ten acres. I am my own boss and doing well. . . ."[10]

That the first anecdote comes from India and the second from Egypt reminds us of what we know in principle but have not always applied in practice the past twenty years—participation is the distinguishing characteristic of modernizing governments. But participation is not synonomous with democracy. It can be achieved in any "modern" political system. The most important difference between countries is not their forms of government. The realities of development at the grass roots level may have little to do with the forms of the political super-structure. The largest democracy in the world, India, the military dictatorship of Brazil, and the socialist state of Burma all fit into the category of dual societies because new forms of superstructure have been grafted on to traditional societies without affecting the essential relationships between rulers and ruled. Elections, where they are held, may simply be a way of ratifying the power of the elite. On the other hand, the modernizing countries that will be cited throughout the book as examples of how really rapid economic growth can be achieved, run the gamut from democratic Israel and Puerto Rico, to communist Yugoslavia, to authoritarian Taiwan, Egypt, and Korea.

Leaving aside the political character of the authoritarian governments, there is no small irony in the fact that the local institutions used by the modernizing authoritarian states to involve the people in development are essentially the same as the local institutions functioning in the successful democracies of the West.

In Yugoslavia, for example, the major function of the 571 commune (county) councils is to plan and carry out local development activities in a number of fields which are traditional functions of local government in the democracies—road networks, land improvement, education and vocational training, utilities, public health, city planning, building codes, social services, and so forth. The communes have wide powers of taxation, supplemented by grants-in-aid and loans from the national government. What the councils possess is the power to make operational decisions within the framework of national policies and stand-ards of technical and administrative performance set by Belgrade. Council members are elected, and the councils hire their own staff. At one time the councils coordinated the investment plans of the factories within their area. However, much of their power over industrial investment was transferred to the Workers' Councils because Belgrade felt the commune councils were channeling too high a proportion of factory profits into nonincome producing activities. To achieve what Yugoslavia calls "social self-management and direct democracy, wide participation among the populace has of course been encouraged. Accordingly, an impressive variety of committees, commissions, citizens' councils, public boards, and other bodies now exist for this purpose. These are buttressed by voters' meetings, which provide the citizen with an increasingly larger role in local government and public affairs. These local citizens' bodies also tend to move toward somewhat open discussion *as long as fundamentals are left alone—that is, as long as no direct challenge to central authority and socialist foundations exist.* . . . The commune together with the workers' council represents the 'grass roots' institution of decentralization which gives Yugoslav socialism its somewhat unique character."[11]

In Taiwan the characteristics and functions of the local governments are similar to Yugoslavia. The now famous Farmers' Associations are, as we shall see later in Chapter 5, viable cooperative business organizations.

In most countries, however, the traditional inhibitions to development continue. To understand better the plight of the mass of marginal people, and also the disappointing record of democratic government, let us examine further some of the characteristics of traditional societies.

From Traditional Societies to
Government by Benevolence

Peasant communities have achieved a remarkably stable accommodation to their environment. The ingenuity of peasant farmers is evidenced by the wide variety of farming systems responding to different environmental conditions around the world. One of the fundamental characteristics of these systems helps to explain the enormous communications gap between the educated and the villagers: they are based on the lore and logic of nature, the knowledge base for accommodating to the environment at low and static levels of productivity. But development today is based on applied science, the knowledge base for modifying the environment for man's benefit at high and rising levels of productivity.

The essentially static outlook on life inherent in this knowledge base of peasant agriculture is encouraged by both ruling elites and farmers in traditional communities. To farmers, innovation is risky. People living at or just above the level of subsistence are reluctant to experiment with new methods when failure could mean hunger or even starvation.

Ruling elites discourage innovation because it can alter the power relationships within a community and hence the whole basis of traditional stability. In the developed countries people have come to accept change as almost inevitable. But in traditional societies there is no such attitude. Innovation is an exception to the normal pattern of life and such innovation as does take place is subsumed by privileged elites. Thus, a farmer who exercises his own initiative and who may, for example, grow a better crop than his neighbors, may find himself the target of traditional sanctions, such as witchcraft. Or, as one frustrated innovator ended his story: "When the ordinary man suddenly makes his will conspicuous, the extortioner (in this case, the local policeman) is on his trail."[1 2]

The elite groups in traditional societies maintain their power by gathering tribute from the rest of the community, generally in the form of surplus agricultural produce and labor. In return for the tribute, they bear certain responsibilities for the community. These typically include such things as protection in time of war or help at a time of personal calamity, such as a death in the family. The elite also may organize work parties to build roads or flood control embankments; they may be the channel for prayers to the gods, or they may be responsible for rain or other ritual responsibilities necessary to maintain the cement of the society.

The manner in which the governing elites gather their tribute and carry out their obligations requires some explanation because the particular practices involved are similar to what Westerners call "corruption." These practices, however, are not considered "corrupt" in traditional communities.

For example, in administering the land tax, there is considerable variation in the rates according to the quality of the land, the crops grown, and, in irrigated areas, the amount of water used. Such a system is designed to make the taxpayer dependent on the "good will" of the tax collector. At the local level it is in the interest of the taxpayer to "bribe" the tax collector to underestimate the amount of high quality land, or the area planted to a high tax rate crop, or the amount of water used in order to reduce his tax payments.

In such a system it is simply assumed that at each level of the government, officials will keep a portion of the tax collections for themselves. These "extra" portions are their salary, for officials are not salaried in this kind of system.

Further, in such a society many official acts, such as issuing permits, which are now called "public services," are done as "favors" in the context of what we call "bribery," rather than as a duty performed for a fixed fee. In principle these services are an expression of the governing elite's interest in the welfare of the people. What actually happens is that the "cost" of the "service" is negotiated between the local official and the villager. After the service is performed, this amount is pocketed by the official rather than deposited in the public treasury.

Officials are not required to perform these services for all people equally, in accordance with written law. If an official chooses not to act, there is virtually no way in which ordinary people can obtain redress. Rather, the "services" are used to reward those who are obedient, compel wanted patterns of behavior, and restrain unwanted initiative.

Thus, actions which seem to us to be forms of "corruption"—bribery, extortion, embezzlement, and nepotism—are actually the nature of the relationship between government and people in a traditional society. They are, in fact, the discipline of such a society, the principal way in which those who rule keep the mass of the people under their control.

In this ritualistic setting, the mass of the poor are expected to display an attitude of conspicuous subservience to their benefactors. Villagers have been conditioned to believe that salvation for their crises comes from the ruling groups, provided that they maintain the proper relationship with them. This is another aspect of the relationship emphasizing dependence of the many upon the few. If, for example, there has been an epidemic of animal disease, and more than the average number of bullocks has died, the villager will say to a government official, "All our bullocks have fallen over and we cannot plough our fields. Send us bullocks or we will surely die."

This is the heritage of government in dual societies where it is assumed that tomorrow will be a repetition of yesterday, where "he who was born to a pot, doesn't leave the kitchen."[13] In this situation, "the government should do something about it," or the negative, "nothing can be done about it," is the attitude of those who believe they are unable to improve their lot in life or that they are not allowed to try.

Thus far, the principal effect of development on the governing elites has been the introduction of a series of programs which we shall describe as government by benevolence—so-called "local" development programs in which the power of decision is retained by central officials; poor relief is disguised as agricultural credit; farmer cooperatives are dominated by officials or local elites; local governments are often actually the local office of the central government rather than government "of, by, and for" the people of the local community, and other characteristics which will be discussed in succeeding chapters. The number of officials needed to manage these programs has had to be increased enormously. Hence, there is now much more government "presence" in local communities than in earlier times, but the relationship between government and people remains essentially unchanged.

These officials also receive tribute and reciprocate by dispensing favors and gifts. As explained above, these practices should not be confused with what we call "corruption." Granting, however, that the significance of these practices is different from similar practices we describe as "corruption," they nevertheless must be removed. They are, to paraphrase Winston Churchill, 'ancient inhibitions that obstruct the adventurous.'[14]

The idea also lingers on that a society is divided between a few who are born to rule and the many who are born to be ruled. In the view of officials the mass of the people are not capable of doing things for themselves. As a result, development plans for local communities are created by the central government. In spite of the diversity of local problems and local situations, uniform solutions are imposed nationwide. Implementation is then passed downwards through a hierarchy of central government bureaucrats.

Some countries, partly in response to Western criticism of excessive centralization of their underdeveloped governments, have decentralized their systems of administration. Such decentralization may appear to bring the government closer to the people, may appear to make the government more responsive to the people's needs because the central official is now located in a field office rather than the national capital. In fact, decentralization of administration does not increase participation or create new opportunities if the people remain unorganized and if the government retains the power of decision.

Government by benevolence is popular among ruling elites because it is a way in which the central government arranges for the people to receive some of the benefits of technological progress which are, in truth, needed for development— roads, schools, dispensaries, fertilizer, and so forth. It thus appears to be modernizing in its results. On the other hand, government by benevolence enables officials to guide the decision process down to the village level. The marginal people continue to be unheard and unheeded. This is why government by benevolence cannot induce the "sustained activity" which is essential for rapid economic progress, and why government by benevolence cannot induce "a sense of belonging," or loyalty—the problem in Vietnam.

Further, North American and European economists have unwittingly reinforced government by benevolence by economic policies (discussed in chapters 3 and 4) which favor control of innovation and investment by the upper income groups.

At this stage, we should perhaps remember a dictum of an earlier age: "a state which dwarfs its men, in order that they may be more docile instruments in its hands, even for beneficial purposes—will find that with small men no great thing can really be accomplished."[15]

Table 1-1 lists important characteristics of dual and modernizing societies that will be discussed in this book. In the real world the difference between the two types of societies is not always as clear-cut as the table suggests. Sometimes the difference is more a matter of degree than of kind. However, table 1-1 is a quick way of indicating major issues of development and the significance of participation in development.

Table 1-1
Important Characteristics of Dual and Modernizing Societies

	Dual	Modernizing
Characteristics of Local Governments and Other Local Organizations		
Organized problem-solving system	Inadequate	Adequate
Decision-making authority	Nominal	Considerable
Financial resources	Limited, essentially static	Considerable and rising
Written records (for both public and individual use)	Rare, not increasing; people rely on memory	Considerable and increasing; reliance on memory declining
Leadership positions	Few; number not increasing much	Many; number increasing
Planned effort to induce transfer of loyalties from traditional to new institutions	No	Yes
Concept of local development	Individual, *ad hoc* projects; little emphasis on interrelationships	Systems and networks; interrelationships emphasized
Organization of Space for Economic Activities		
Organizes market towns	No	Yes
Investment in infrastructure (electricity, transport, storage, land improvement)		
National systems	Adequate	Adequate
Regional systems	Tends to be adequate	Adequate
Local systems	Inadequate; often nonnetwork	Adequate, built as networks

Table 1-1 (cont.)

Build linkages between national, regional, and local levels	Unsystematic and slow	Essentially systematic and rapid
Policy, Attitudes, Trends Related to Production System		
Government believes the poor can pay cost of own improvement	No	Yes
Price system	Substantial administrative controls	Strong reliance on "the market"
"Efficiency" generally equated with "bigness" and the "latest machines"	Yes	No
Subsidized capital investment (which benefits mostly the rich)	Considerable	Little
Geographic dispersion of industry	Some	Considerable
Systematic extension of the financial system to local level	No	Yes
Support of small producers	Little	Much
Number of investors	Few; increasing slowly	Few in the beginning; rising rapidly
Income distribution	Inequality increasing	Inequality decreasing
Un- and underemployment	Rising	Falling
Tenancy and/or land reform	Lip service; lax enforcement	Enforced
Agricultural taxation (land and incomes)	Low	Generally high
Education		
Rely on formal education system	Yes	Yes
Willingness to introduce variety of "non-formal" education programs	Little	Much
"The Population Explosion"		
Birth rates	High and essentially static	Falling
Exports (Per Capita)	Rising slowly, static, or falling	Rising rapidly

Organization and Participation

The solution of the problem of those who for centuries have been "wholly over-looked" begins with organization. Hence, the first step in development is to organize the mass of the people in relatively autonomous local institutions and to link these institutions with higher levels of the economy and the society. People can be expected to invest in a modern economy only when they believe they are part of it and can benefit from it.

But there remains the difficult problem of defining the relationship between these local organizations and democracy—giving citizens a free choice of their leaders and policies at the national level. It is tempting to quote de Tocqueville as a guide to combining the modernization process with political freedom: "Local assemblies of citizens constitute the strength of free nations. Town meetings are to liberty what primary schools are to science; they bring it within reach; they teach men how to use it and how to enjoy it. A nation may establish a system of free government, but without the spirit of municipal institutions, it cannot have the spirit of liberty."[16]

While it is true that "local assemblies" and decentralization are characteristics of free societies of the West, their existence is no guarantee that a society is free, at least in the sense we use the term in the West. Participation is not synonymous with democratic government. Rather, participation, including a "sense of belonging," is the distinguishing characteristic of modernizing governments. It is precisely because the mass of the people have been the "victims" rather than the "beneficiaries" of politics that modernizing authoritarian governments can succeed.

The situation of a farmer who now owns his own land and is a member (and could be elected an officer) of a local cooperative that possesses some autonomy is an enormous advance over a situation in which the landlord could commit a capital crime with impunity—the circumstance described by the Egyptian farmer earlier in this chapter. Perhaps the best measure of the significance of participation and decentralization, from the point of view of the poor, is the ability of modernizing authoritarian governments not just to endure, but to induce some measure of popular support as well.

One of the great ironies of the twentieth century is that it is the modernizing authoritarian governments which understand the importance of organizing people. "The ability to create public organizations and political institutions is in short supply today. It is this ability which, above all else, the communists offer modernizing countries."[17] Even Mao Tse-tung's peasant version of Marxism is, in considerable measure, an organizational strategy. We democrats, however, have been economic determinists vis-a-vis the Third World. We have assumed that increasing economic growth would, almost automatically, increase participation and social justice. These latter ideas were supposed to be implemented through the democratic superstructure imposed on the poor countries as they were emerging into independence. But the democratic superstructure has generally not provided greater opportunity and access for the mass of the poor. One consequence is that economic growth rates have been lower than is needed to alleviate poverty.

In our view the future of democracy is, indeed, bleak if current trends in the dual societies continue. The modernizing societies, with their emphasis on participation, are at least building a viable base from which more humane societies can evolve. This could include workable democratic forms, though we need to remember that democracy as we understand it, is clearly not the same kind of democracy that might evolve in other cultures and traditions.

The question underlying the book, then, is whether the Western democracies can help the poor nations, initially, to organize people to participate in development, and subsequently, to help them institutionalize "a respect for the preciousness of human life." Any role the rich democracies can play depends on political decisions made in the poor countries.

Hence, this book will concentrate on ideas that can be used in the poor countries if the latter want to achieve broad-based development. In the final chapter we shall reconsider the relationship between the rich and poor countries in what should be a partnership in development rather than the superior-inferior status implied in the common phrase, foreign aid.

2 Organizing People

If broad-based development as defined in the first chapter is to proceed, it will require that the people of the poor countries be organized within an institutional framework that gives them access to the national economic and social systems. This organization is a political act because it alters the distribution of power within the community by increasing the number of people who are making decisions. These decisions will be taken not only in the field of national politics as narrowly conceived, but in a wide range of other organizations, such as farmers' organizations, trade unions, business enterprises, professional associations, and many others.

One can reasonably ask why a government should consciously set out to alter the power base on which it is established. The essential reason lies in the strength and appeal of a set of ideas regarding the relationship between government and people: the ideas which transformed once feudal Europe are stirring men's minds everywhere. These ideas have already brought about the independence of all but a handful of the former colonial countries. They have made broad-based development an imperative of our time.

Governments should expand their power base because "development is much more than a matter of encouraging economic growth within a given social structure. It is rather the modernization of that structure, a process of ideational, social, economic, and political change that requires the remaking of society in its most intimate as well as its most public attributes."[1]

This quotation implies that economic growth is not a sufficient definition of development. Rather, the modernization of a society involves a restructuring of relationships between government and people so that the mass of the people can exercise some influence over national policies that affect their own lives.

In traditional societies an individual's status and relationship with other people is determined primarily by one criterion—birth. But in a modernizing society the status of an individual and his relationships with other people is influenced by a number of new systems and institutions: money and banking, the market, the law of contracts, the corporation, the law of property, local government, savings and credit systems, the cooperative, the trade union, professional associations, and educational institutions. These and many other institutions and systems are just as much inventions as the steam engine or the iron smelter. They are just as necessary for development as the products of the assembly line.

The second reason the power base needs to be expanded is that dual society governments may not endure unless the ruling elites are willing to bridge the gap

17

between themselves and the marginal masses. It is true, to be sure, that there are still very many dual society governments in existence. But the Age of Development (since World War II) has been characterized by an extraordinarily high level of political instability throughout the Third World. There have been so many forcible changes of government in the last quarter century that this period of history might also be called the Age of *Coups d'État*. During the few months in which this book was being written there were successful *coups* in Turkey, Uganda, Bolivia, Thailand and Dahomey, unsuccessful attacks upon the government in Ceylon, Morocco, Sudan, both successful and unsuccessful attacks in Argentina, and the separation of Bangladesh from Pakistan.

"A state without the means of some change is without the means of its conservation."[2] The state can be conserved only if people believe they belong to it, that because of their own personal interests they have a stake in its survival. If a state is to create a sense of belonging among the great mass of the people, then it must decentralize the decision-making process, not just in politics but in an array of human endeavor. Relative political stability combined with economic progress can only be achieved over a sustained period by modernizing societies as opposed to dual societies.

What the modernizing states have grasped is that decentralization is a way of creating a "sense of belonging," of extending the limit of peoples' confidence outward and upward from the traditional tiny world of their village to the much larger world of their district, their region, their country. The problem in many Third World countries is that governments, far from viewing decentralization as a way of winning the support of the people, view it as a loss of control, a splintering and weakening of the political system. What is needed is an understanding of how decentralization can be used both to stimulate local initiative and strengthen central governments.

Before discussing how the successful countries have combined these two fundamental aspects of modern government, we should perhaps note that the United States has tended to ignore the central problem of politics in the developing countries. That problem was solved such a long time ago in our own country that we hardly have occasion to think about it. And, from our knowledge of the despotisms of history, we are taught from an early age to be suspicious of political power and those who exercise it.

However, the very first thing to be said about the United States Constitution is that it represents the creation and diffusion of political power. It created a government which possesses the power to govern. It allows people to participate in public affairs. The separation of powers, civil rights, and other means of controlling the abuse of power, however necessary to sustain freedom, are nevertheless secondary matters. Because our Founding Fathers created a government that possesses the power to govern, we have rightly been more concerned with the control of political power than with the creation of political power.

In the Third World, however, many governments do not possess the power to govern. They are unable to adjust to the change which is the very nature of the modernizing process. The creation and diffusion of sufficient political power to enable governments to govern is the great political problem of development.

Typically, the political base in the poor countries is limited to a handful of traditional elites plus a small number of newcomers—factory owners, merchants, professional people, skilled workers. Politics is not motivated by some set of ideas which can be supported by people of all ranks, but by personal allegiances that are ever shifting as the few who are allowed to participate continuously try to outmaneuver each other. The ease and frequency with which governments are overthrown tell us that politics is fragile when it lacks roots in the problems, hopes, and loyalties of people. The very concept of development, that it is "the evolution of a different art of living and working together,"[3] has made traditional politics obsolete. Governments can no longer govern effectively unless they extend some measure of recognition to those who have long gone unheard and unheeded.

In oversimple terms the organization of a modern political system is a problem of relationships between different levels of government. The central government no longer tries to control the decision-making process down to the village level. Rather, the central government organizes relatively autonomous regional and local organizations to solve development problems appropriate to each level.

The delegation of substantial decision-making authority does not mean that local authorities are free to do as they wish. "The central government is alert both to restrain and stimulate. The control of the central over the local government is threefold—judicial, legislative, and administrative. Local authorities are in no real sense autonomous; if they exceed their powers or neglect their duties, they may find themselves in conflict with the law, with Parliament, or with one or more central administrative departments."[4] Although this statement was originally written about Britain, this combination—"to restrain and stimulate"—is the nature of the relationship between the central government and local organizations in modernizing states.

The art of organizing people lies in allowing decisions to be made at the appropriate level—national, regional, or local—thus allowing the diverse needs of the smaller communities to be embraced within a broader and uniform national policy. The political scientist calls this the creation of a "fusion of national and local interest." If this fusion can be achieved, then local and regional communities can come to feel an integral part of a larger system, rather than feeling that they are "wholly overlooked." If, however, "local interest" is not created, if the central bureaucracy controls decisions and implementation down to the local level, then the "revolution of rising expectations" is likely to coincide with "falling satisfactions."

When decisions are made centrally, they tend to be based on superficial observation and what appears to be common sense from the point of view of the central bureaucracy. But this is not sufficient to solve problems at the local level.

It may seem a matter of common sense to build a road between two villages where no road exists. But what the villagers need is not just a road here and a bridge there. What they need is a local transport network which is linked to a regional transport network which, in turn, is tied in to the national network.

Building a local transport network requires a system for collecting and analyzing facts, planning development programs, determining priorities, making decisions and implementing them. The same point applies to all sectors of development: agriculture, industry, education, and so forth. It applies also to coordination of projects between sectors so that, for example, there will be sufficient roads to carry the fertilizer from factory to farm and, in turn, to transport from farm to market the increased production which fertilizer makes possible. In addition, the same point applies to the relationship between different levels of the economy. In transport, electric power, distribution of fertilizer, marketing, and a host of other development activities, rapid economic progress requires that viable local organizations be tied in to the national system. In a broader social sense, these linkages are needed if a person is to believe that in developing his local community he is helping to build his country.

It is a combination of local decision-making authority and an ever increasing capacity of local groups to apply modern science to carry out their own decisions that distinguishes modernizing societies from dual societies. Thus modernizing societies have succeeded in delegating authority so that problems are solved at a level appropriate to the nature of the problem. One effect of delegation, in addition to its political value discussed above, is to erode the traditional belief that man is the victim of his environment. Modernizing governments have recognized that people cannot believe they have the power to exercise control over their environment unless they are able to understand and use the means of control in the routine activities of everyday life.

We can then identify three essential and complementary elements of a problem-solving system:

1. A decision-making system, which allows decisions to be made at the appropriate level
2. A system of building a knowledge base for the masses and making it accessible to all so that decisions will be based on applied knowledge and experience
3. Effective linkages between different levels of the system

These are all conspicuously lacking in the dual society countries. Governments and development assistance agencies have long recognized the lack of problem solving experience and capacity in local communities in dual societies. So far, however, most of the programs intended to organize and energize the people have not incorporated the three crucial elements of a problem-solving system. To illustrate the organizational deficiencies of government by benevolence, we shall discuss the first, and, for many years, the largest program that was supposedly intended to modernize dual societies—Traditional Community Development (TCD).

Organizational Deficiencies of Government by Benevolence

Traditional Community Development programs were started twenty years ago in India and the Philippines and then spread throughout Asia and much of Africa. The west coast countries of South America picked it up about the same time the Alliance for Progress was organized. During the 1950s TCD was strongly supported by several of the aid agencies, foremost among them the American agency.

The proponents of Traditional Community Development expected the program to induce both an agricultural revolution and the beginnings of rural democracy. By the mid-1960s, however, TCD was on the wane because no country using it was making rapid progress toward either objective. The other way round, the modernizing countries have not used TCD as a local development program. Even so, at the same time TCD was declining throughout much of the Third World, the most lavish program of the past two decades was being sponsored by our own country—in South Vietnam.[a]

The principle behind the TCD programs is to initiate development in individual villages on the basis of what the people perceive to be their felt needs. TCD is customarily initiated by sending into the village a specially trained civil servant known as the multipurpose Village Level Worker (VLW). By living in the village and working with the villagers, he is expected to gain their confidence. By talking with them, making suggestions and organizing discussions, the VLW is supposed to help the villagers identify their felt needs. However, the government does not trust the people with the power of decision. Rather, "a decision on what projects should be assisted must be left to the community development worker."[5]

What is wrong with this program? In the first place, it lacks the central characteristics of a decision-making system. The "feelings" of the villagers are no substitute for the collection and analysis of facts. Furthermore, there was little sense of system or priorities in TCD. Whether the villagers "felt" they should build a road, a primary school, or a well has been a matter of indifference to central officials. It has simply been assumed that one project would lead to another and that somehow, over a period of time, a number of individual projects in individual villages would turn into a road system, a school system, or a water supply system. But the villagers had little knowledge of the requirements of modern technologies and of the need to establish local systems linked to the

[a]Where it has been known by such names as Revolutionary Development, Pacification, and Village Self-Development.

national system. Further, it has never been made clear in TCD how or when someone, presumably the central government, would decide that the poor had learned how to identify their "felt needs" and therefore would be trusted with the power of decision, that is to say, would be accepted into the system. Finally, the assumption that there can be no advance unless an outsider is inserted into the village community is yet another example of the lack of confidence of dual society governments in the people they rule.

The failure of TCD as a decision-making system is compounded by the arbitrariness of the review process. Action on village proposals does not begin until and unless the proposal is approved by a central civil servant. The local proposals may be revised, but usually the villagers are not told why these changes are made. This process of civil service review may drag on for months. In this circumstance, the villager is not certain whether he is deciding or recommending, whether he is being trusted or overseen, whether he is planning his own future or simply doing as he is told, as is his centuries-old habit.

Another weakness in TCD decision-making is the lack of a system of recording and retaining information at the local level, which is, of course, an essential part of any effective problem-solving system. Most of the information collected is used by officials to prepare reports to their superiors in the civil service rather than for dissemination among the villagers who need it. The program is not used as a way for the villagers to build up a knowledge base from their experiences.

Finally, the focus of TCD is inward, not outward—the reconstruction of an individual village rather than the reconstruction of rural society. Subsistence societies are atomized societies. The atoms, that is the villages, cannot be modernized individually. Rather, part of the modernization process is linking them with the outside world—socially, politically, and economically. These linkages, which are the third element of a problem-solving system and which are discussed throughout this book, are not a part of TCD programs.

The result of this combination of flaws is that TCD programs have primarily achieved a certain amount of physical progress; especially highly visible effects such as roads, schools, dispensaries and community centers. They fill some of the unsystematic felt needs of the villagers. They also fulfill the obligations of the central government officials to provide tokens of their presence. But they have not provided the villagers with a means of solving their own basic problems. Nor have they brought about what is supposed to be the major purpose of "economic" development—higher incomes. However, a program which emphasizes "amenities before necessities" is interpreted by officials as confirmation of their view that peasants in the poor countries are essentially incapable of doing much for themselves. Traditional Community Development is but one of many programs pursued by dual societies that has not succeeded in providing people the means to help themselves.[6]

Principles of a Problem-Solving System

The key to releasing the energies of the peoples of the poor countries lies in designing effective problem-solving systems. This would admit the marginal people into a world from which they have always been excluded—the world of knowledge and control of their destinies. Unless they are admitted to this world, the prospects for broad-based development and for swift and sustained economic growth are slim, as we shall show in subsequent chapters.

True development involves stimulating the initiative of villagers and the urban poor—countless millions of individual deeds by individual people—by organizing them in disciplined problem-solving institutions which have the authority and the resources to carry out their own decisions. This is possible only if central governments move away from their traditional detailed control over local activities toward policy determination and general supervision. How do central governments do this so that the political system is strengthened and stabilized? On the basis of the experience of the countries that have been successful in achieving this goal, we can identify six principles. Of necessity these can only be expressed in general terms. We must always bear in mind that adaptation and flexibility are required when the principles are put into practice.

Identifying Regional and Local Functions

The first principle is to identify and define the different functions that must be performed at the regional and local levels of a country rather than the national level. The most vital of these functions are described in the remaining chapters of this book. They include the supply of production inputs, such as seeds, fertilizer, and irrigation water for agriculture, together with the marketing and processing of produce, extension of technical knowledge, and credit for farmers and businessmen; a transport network; an electric power system; a variety of local and regional industrial and commercial activities; and certain types of nonformal education programs in addition to the expansion and improvement of the formal school system.

Definition of National Policy Framework

The second principle is that the central government must define the national policy framework in which the numerous problems of development are to be solved and the level at which they should be solved—national, regional, or local. Much of the responsibility for planning and implementation will be delegated to regional or local institutions because much of the work of development should be done at regional and local levels. Central governments should not build farm-to-market roads and they cannot grow food. These regional and local organizations must have sufficient income—from taxes, income-producing activities, grants-in-aid, loans, and so forth—to pay the costs of their own investments.

Chapter 3 will describe the need for the distribution of a network of market towns and intermediate-sized cities throughout the poor countries. In the context of organizing people, the reason for this strategy is that these towns and cities will be the location of the organizations which will be responsible for local planning, decision-making, investing, and the development and dissemination of knowledge. Individual villages will have a role in development programs, but that role will be primarily concerned with the implementation of decisions made one level above the individual village, namely, the township or county. Representatives of individual villages will, of course, be involved in decision-making at this level. As we shall see in chapter 3, the management of local development programs in the successful countries is not located in individual villages but above them.

There are practical reasons for locating local organizations above individual villages. These include cost and the lack of trained personnel. No central government can afford the number of trained people, such as agricultural extension agents, that would be required on a one per village basis in the manner in which some central governments actually tried to place one VLW in each village in TCD programs. If, for example, India tried to train enough agricultural extension agents to have one per village, she would need three times as many agents per 1000 farmers as there are in the Western countries or Japan. Not even the United States is rich enough to support all the different kinds of technically trained people needed for development, if development is organized around individual villages.[7]

However, the more important reasons for organizing above the individual village involve the relationship between government and people. The notion that progress in the village cannot be initiated unless an outsider is sent into it was interpreted by villagers as another example of central government condescension to which they have become inured through the centuries. In recent times the purpose of sending the outsider into the village has been different and more benevolent than the traditional purposes of collection of taxes or conscription of young men for the military and large-scale public works projects. But the change in purpose of the outsider has not altered the condescending relationship between government and people.

The fact is that outsiders must enter the village. Especially in the early stages of development, technically trained personnel must be provided by the government, for there is no other source. The problem is to devise a working relationship between official personnel and the villagers that is acceptable to the latter.

It is crucial that the outside technician should not be planted directly in the village, for this represents an invasion of the privacy of the community. Development involves change in the most intimate and personal relationships among human beings—in individuals, in extended families, in local factions, in the village community. An outsider in the village, far from inducing the informal and personal changes in human relationships and attitudes that are the most fundamental aspect of development, inhibits them. There are many things which villagers will neither do nor say in the presence of a stranger, especially if he represents the government. These changes must take place in the privacy of one's self and one's community, or they will not take place at all.

How can a technician induce ideas for change, while at the same time being responsive and responsible to the local community? This combination can be achieved by having the central officials work at the county or township with the officers of the local government, the farmer cooperatives, and other township or county organizations rather than directly with the villagers in the village. The point is easily stated. It is the psychology of the relationship which requires further explanation.

Under modernizing policies we assume relatively autonomous local organizations which have been delegated the responsibility for designated local activities and which are developing their own problem-solving capacities. In the new system the role of central officials is to help, to train, to suggest, perhaps to apply pressure—but not to exercise detailed control over local activities. From the point of view of the villagers, the initiators of change are no longer outsiders but themselves and the officers of their own organizations. Hence, when the central official enters the village, he enters as the agent of the local organization, not the agent of the suspect central government. His purpose is no longer to carry out instructions handed down from above, but to carry out instructions approved and issued by the people with whom he is working.

In practice, the difference in how a central official enters the village under dual society and modernizing systems is not quite so clear-cut as expressed here. The point to emphasize is that the local people must feel they have some recourse against actions or recommendations of central officials with which they do not agree. Creating local organizational strength is the beginning of this recourse.

Setting Minimum Standards of Performance

The third principle is that central governments must set minimum standards of performance and enforce them through supervision, inspection, auditing the accounts (and jailing the embezzlers), and by imposing sanctions if the standards are not met. The central government must assure that modernizing institutions are operated for the benefit of the community. Otherwise, traditional elites will manage them for their own benefit. In India, for example, "the result, typically and plainly, has been to lodge the village cooperative in the hands of the same privileged village cliques that have been doing most of the traditional money-lending and trading. By insisting on the pretense of indigenous origin (i.e., the village), the forces of reform have surrendered the cooperative instrument to management by the very groups most inclined to resist massive rural reconstruction. In the process, the primary (local) cooperative society has tended to become simply another device for reinforcing the pattern of rural privilege—with the comfortable new feature of a direct line of credit on the Reserve Bank of India."[8]

However, in Taiwan, "The government . . . insisted that all farmers associations should prepare annual programs of work, together with budgets, and saw to it that they were satisfactorily carried out."[9] In addition, the government assured that all farmers had access to the means of production, the financial system, the market, and knowledge on approximately equal terms. By such actions, the central government can curb the abuse of power at the local level and protect the rights of the individual. By retaining overall policy control over local activities, it augments the fusion of local and national interest because farmers can see a direct relationship between their own local development activities and government policy.

A Local Problem—Solving System

The fourth principle is that the central government must introduce a modern problem-solving system at the local level so that the mass of the people can learn how to solve technological problems. That the people have virtually no training and no experience in problem-solving is a secondary reason why central governments are reluctant to decentralize. They fear that local decisions will be unreasonable or uneconomic, or resources will be wasted. The answer to this problem is not, however, for central governments to continue making decisions for the people, but rather to organize a system in which people can learn through their own experience. Central governments are not wise enough "to govern from a distance." No central bureaucracy, even in the developed countries, has the administrative capacity to make the infinite multitude of decisions which development requires.

One of the problems with the establishment of new local institutions is that, without care, they may be usurped by the traditional elites, and so become forces of the status quo. Yet, in Taiwan, Egypt, and Comilla County,[b] in Bangladesh, many of the local leaders, such as the officers of the farmer cooperatives or

---

[b]The discussion in this book of the Comilla rural development project pertains to the period when Bangladesh was still East Pakistan. The future of the Comilla project was still uncertain at the time the book was completed.

the local government, are ex-landlords, ex-moneylenders, ex-traders—the very same group of traditional elites who are blamed for the lack of progress elsewhere. How do we reconcile the very different type of performance—leadership for change and leadership against change—by similar groups of people in different countries?

Part of the answer has already been discussed—establishing minimum standards of performance, creating the conditions of access for small producers, organizing viable local governments, cooperatives, and other local institutions, and removing the level of the problem-solving organization to the township or country, above the level of traditional village factions. There are two more principles of local development which help to explain how the process of gradual reform can be implanted in essentially static situations.

Leadership Positions

The number of leadership positions should exceed the number of traditional leaders. There are both practical and social reasons for applying this principle. On the practical side, the amount of work which must be done to modernize traditional rural societies is enormous and much more than can be managed by the very small number of traditional leaders who have maintained their positions, in part, by limiting sharply the number of leadership positions in their communities. In Taiwan, for example, some 6 percent of the regular members of the Farmers Associations hold an elected position in the Association. Another 3 percent are members of village extension committees. Other villagers are officers in the local government, irrigation associations, the farm tenancy committees, and other local organizations both official and voluntary. In addition, there are 13 "demonstration farm-households" per township and a larger number of demonstration fields (on farmers', not government, land).[10] In the beginning there were not enough traditional leaders to fill all these positions.

But the more important reasons behind this principle are social. The creation of large numbers of leadership positions is one way of beginning to loosen up the stratified social structures that are characteristic of traditional societies. The positions are commonly filled through elections, even in authoritarian countries. In the beginning these elections are not the free choice elections of democratic theory. Rather, they are simply a way of endorsing the individuals nominated by extended families or village factions to represent them. It takes some period of time, of work well done and badly done, of comparing notes with acquaintances in neighboring communities before people begin to realize that leaders should be judged on the basis of performance as well as kinship or factional loyalty.

New leadership positions represent the kind of new opportunities that need to be created in the rigid social structures of traditional villages. The new positions are a way of subjecting traditional leaders to competition. But most important of all, the application of this principle confronts the traditional leaders with a choice. Either they must become leaders of development or run the risk of losing their positions. If we may judge on the basis of the few countries which have applied this principle, many of the traditional leaders will choose to become leaders of development rather than give up their positions of prestige and authority in their communities. In their new role, the people will continue to accept their leadership. Hence, in the leadership principle we find one of the keys to gradual and peaceful change in the social system.

The failure to apply the leadership position principle is one of the reasons why the poor record of the local governments, cooperatives, and other local organizations, can be blamed on traditional leaders in many countries. It is also yet another of the defects of programs such as Traditional Community Development. In most societies only one new leadership position was created through TCD programs, the Village Level Worker. Even this position was preempted by the government, for the VLW was a central civil servant. Most traditional societies have some sort of a village council or council of elders, which can be traced back into the dim past. Hence, the use of these councils in TCD programs did not involve the wholesale creation of new leadership positions. Even where councils were reorganized or enlarged, which was done in a few countries, the number of new positions created was small. TCD is actually a way of strengthening traditional elites by expanding their responsibilities without subjecting them to new standards of performance or competition. Hence, the leadership principle is a vital part of initiating the process of reform in village society without also inducing violent disruption.

Transferring Loyalty to Modernizing
Institutions

The new institutions that are established outside and above the level of the individual village must contain sufficient incentives to induce a gradual transfer of loyalty from traditional to modernizing institutions.

The ancient institutions, such as the extended family, village factions, and the council of elders, tend to be negative and constrictive. One of their purposes is to enforce at the local level the restraints upon participation, voluntary leadership, opportunity, and initiative that are characteristic of traditional societies. They are "ancient inhibitions that obstruct the adventurous." These institutions are also designed to reduce, very nearly to zero, the village's contacts with the outside world.

The new institutions are intended to enlarge the very small world in which the villager lives. Factions and kinship ties, which seem so overwhelming in the small confines of a village, are submerged in the larger community of a township or county. Gradually villagers will come to realize that the interests of a community larger than the village are more important than traditional extended family and factional ties that inhibit their self-improvement. Villagers will learn, for example, that the local irrigation system can only follow the contours of the land, not the contours of traditional factions.

The new institutions are intended also to give the mass of ordinary people a variety of new opportunities, such as leadership, mentioned above. And economic opportunity should be present from the start: it can be created by giving people access to the means of production, the financial system, the market, and knowledge. For example, whereas the villager may well be denied agricultural credit in the traditional village, he can have access to credit in the modernizing institutions.[c]

Finally, new groupings of people will appear that cut across traditional factional and kinship ties—economic, professional, social, educational, sports, youth, women, and others. Gradually, people will be drawn together in these different combinations by a new set of common purposes and common needs.

The task of governments is to create new institutions and new incentives. But governments cannot force the pace of change. People will gradually transfer some of their loyalties only as they reconcile in their own minds the conflicts between traditional and modernizing values and attitudes. If the incentives are strong enough, this change will take place. In Taiwan, for example, the ideal family is no longer the extended family of tradition but a much smaller combination of grandparents, parents, and unmarried children.[11]

These six principles, taken together, form the basis of a system for organizing people to solve their own problems. They create decision-making institutions at a local level and link them to regional and national institutions. In so doing they provide for the systematic accumulation of knowledge in local communities and begin to loosen up the social structure.

To complete our chapter on principles of organizing people, we include a description of how one country—Taiwan—has established local problem-solving bodies to carry out national agricultural policies:

The Government sets its policies and maps out a plan for agricultural development. Sound and realistic as such a plan may be, it will be of little use if it is not put into execution efficiently and thoroughly with the active support and full participation of the people at the grass roots level. Considering the great gap between the national government and individual farmers, the need is apparent for some field organizations to act as a medium to fill that gap and link the national agricultural plan and farmers together. These organizations must, on the one hand, always maintain close contact with farmers and have a profound knowledge of the local agricultural conditions, available resources and farmers' needs so that they can transmit such information to the Government for consideration in its agricultural planning. On the other hand, they must be able to stimulate and develop the initiative and self-help spirit of farmers so that the latter can readily be called upon to respond to the national Plan in the direction where

[c]Farm credit is discussed in chapter 5, nonfarm credit in chapter 6.

their efforts are needed. In Taiwan, this intermediate role in agricultural development is played by township offices, farmers' associations, and irrigation associations.

The township office is at the bottom of the pyramid of the government structure in Taiwan and constitutes the basic unit of local administration. Counterbalancing the powers of the township office is the township council which functions as the voice of local democracy with all its members elected through universal suffrage. Essentially democratic in nature, and with a completely independent public finance, the township office is an important link in the island's administrative chain, leading to higher levels of government at one end, and maintaining physical contact with and serving directly the people at the other. Agriculture is an important phase of the work of the township office which not only participates in the national agricultural planning, but is responsible for the implementation of the agricultural program with which the particular township is concerned.

The farmers' association is a nongovernmental cooperative society organized by the farmers themselves. It is dedicated to the promotion of farmers' interests, advancement of farming techniques and knowledge, improvement of rural living conditions, and development of the rural economy. Being the farmers' own organization and with adequate resources and physical facilities at its disposal, it is in a position to find out the real needs of its members and provide the means to meet their needs. It is organized at three levels: provincial, county, and township. At present, there are one provincial association, 22 county associations, and 324 township associations, forming a complete pyramidal pattern from the supervisory and advisory down to the operational level. The operational level of farmers' associations is the township level. The service activities of a farmers' association include cooperative marketing and processing of farm products, purchasing of farm supplies, extension of farm loans and acceptance of deposits, distribution of fertilizers, and the sponsoring of agricultural extension service and other rural welfare services. These activities are related directly to agricultural production and farmers' life and, most important of all, they are geared to the government efforts for agricultural and rural improvements.

There are altogether 26 irrigation associations in Taiwan. They are also formed on a district basis and controlled by the farmers themselves. The main functions of an irrigation association are the management, maintenance and improvement of irrigation and drainage facilities; regulation and control of water in canals; settlement of water disputes; and land improvement and soil conservation. It also assists in the planning and implementation of regional irrigation projects in cooperation with government agencies. Irrigation is an essential factor in agricultural production. It is largely through the efforts of these local voluntary groups that the vast network of irrigation systems in Taiwan has been properly maintained, utilized and further improved.[17]

3 Organizing a National Economy

We have looked briefly at some of the successes and failures in the development process, and also at some of the most significant lessons that have been learned about organizing a populace so that the great majority can participate in that process. In this chapter we shall examine the outline of a national economic framework that can overcome the major drawbacks to the organization of a modern production system in a dual society.[1]

Progress in a dual society is like an oasis in the desert. Its benefits tend to accrue to the elite groups who live comfortably while surrounded by a desert of poverty. And the situation tends to perpetuate itself. In historical terms, we can see what has been happening.

Because the industrialized nations were taken as the models of development, industrialization and self-sufficiency became the ideal in the plans of most poor countries. Much capital was therefore invested in industries that produced goods to replace imports. These industries were meant primarily to service the needs of the market, which in most countries meant the rather small urban elite of government officials, businessmen, and those few workers who were employed in modern industry and so received good wages. Most of these people lived in the capital of the country and in the few other large cities. Thus, the hidden lure of import substitution as a basis for industrialization lay in the existing urban market. As a result, the industries tended to concentrate in the big cities, where they were also closer to the bureaucracies on whom they depended for their lifelines—licenses, import tariffs, and so on.

Most of these industries, in their infancy, were heavily protected from outside competition by tariffs and quotas. They could therefore afford the luxuries of inefficiency and underuse of capacity. At the same time, profits for the new domestic manufactures did not depend upon market development but resulted almost automatically from changing the source of supply from foreign to domestic. There has thus been little market development in the poor countries save for the 'natural' expansion of the market in the few urban centers. From this developed the concentration of consumption among the higher income groups in the cities.

It was precisely these elite groups that could afford to consume. The new industries employed modern technologies brought in from the West. They required a lot of capital but provided few jobs. Those workers who obtained jobs had high productivity with the modern equipment. They enjoyed high wages and joined the elite. But this process did not extend very far, principally because the

31

demand for the goods produced by the new industries was restricted to the relatively well-off. There were few linkages to the rest of the economy: the new industries did not increase the demand for indigenous small-scale industrial products; indeed they often served as substitutes. There was little integration of agricultural and industrial development, since the consumer goods factories, geared to the city market, contributed little to the growth of the agricultural sector.

In simple terms, then, a dual economy can be described as containing an elite group consuming the products that it produces for itself and a large majority of the population who are marginal to this process. Most of the industrial development that has occurred has been in the large port cities, or cities which saw their birth as colonial administrative centers. Import substitution usually was initiated in light engineering industries which make consumer goods. It started with the final stage of production, the assembly of components into a completed product, and then moved backwards through the various stages of the production process. Assembly was followed by the local manufacture of production goods needed to produce consumer goods. Since all of these factories were related to each other, their most economic location was next to each other, as long as the bulk of the raw materials or components continued to be imported. Thus, more and more factories tended to be concentrated in the same place.

The infrastructure (roads, power, housing, schools, and so on) in poor nations has tended to follow and reinforce this metropolitan bias. National transport systems, for example, have been concentrated on linking ports with each other and with the inland cities by railway. Electric power generation and transmission patterns have been focused on providing power for the metropolitan centers. And it is the workers in those industries who have generally received the benefits of investments in public housing and schools.

This heavy emphasis on metropolitan investment has implied a consequent neglect of investment in the rest of the economy wherein the great majority of the population must find its living. Largely because of these two factors—the conscious building up of the large cities and the neglect of small industries and agriculture—an enormous number of people have migrated from the countryside to the cities. Over the period 1920 to 1960, the big cities of the Third World mushroomed to eight times their initial size. In the mid-1960s, 1/3 of Bogota's 2 million inhabitants had lived in the city less than five years. And 22 million more people were added to the sprawling, crowded cities of the poor countries in 1971 alone. Indeed, the population of many of the national capitals is growing at 5 or 6 percent a year—which means that they double in size every 12 to 14 years. Perhaps half of this growth comes from natural increases in the urban population, the rest from migration.

This unprecedented urban growth has brought about potentially grave problems. The number of people seeking industrial work is growing much more rapidly than employment opportunities. In Latin America during the 1960s, jobs in industry have only grown by 2.3 percent a year, less than the annual growth rate of the population.[2] This has meant that many millions in the cities are either unemployed (unemployment rates of 10 to 15 percent are common), or they subsist in marginal jobs as petty traders, tourist guides, casual laborers or shoeshine boys. At the same time, the cities are beset by staggering problems of slums, crime, and disease.

Why then are so many millions migrating to the cities? The answer is a complex mixture of urban "pull"—the attraction of higher wages, social, cultural and educational activities, and the glamour of the towns; and rural "push"—the desire to escape from a stagnation that offers unrewarding jobs in an atmosphere devoid of hope. On the economic side, a type of "gold rush fever" afflicts many migrants: it is worth a man's while to go to the city even if he remains unemployed or shines shoes, provided that he has some hope of obtaining a coveted job in modern industry, with security and higher wages.

The dual society that has grown up as a consequence of these trends has been described as follows:

One cannot escape the dichotomy between the new and the old, the scientific and the traditional, the experimental and the fatalistic, the achievement-oriented and the status-dominated. Instead of narrowing and bridging this gap, metropolitan centering (the concentration of development in a few large cities), widens it by tending to polarize the demographic spectrum. Its effect is to gather the progressive elements in the society into metropolitan concentrations that, in terms of income and ideas, pull farther and farther away from the traditional rural mass.[3]

To this, one should add the divergence occurring within the cities between those with good, high-productivity, high-wage jobs and those without.

Need for a National Economy

How long can this situation continue? Not only is there a growing gap between the elites and the masses, but the cities themselves seem likely to be strangled by increased numbers and particularly by the unemployed and underemployed. By using standard demographic techniques, the United Nations once projected a population of as much as 101 million in India's two largest cities by the end of this century—35 million for Bombay and 66 million for Calcutta.[4] Today, the combined population of the two cities is 9 million. It is difficult to imagine that these two cities will actually become such urban monsters. That such a projection is possible is, nevertheless, a measure of the concentration of urbanization when so much of development is located in a handful of big cities. Such projections also imply political and social problems of enormous scale and unknown consequence.

Is there an alternative to these trends? Can the worst inequities in income distribution and power be corrected without slowing the hopes for overall economic growth? Can the rural areas and smaller-scale industries become full partners in the development process so as to prevent the strangulation of the cities? The answer to these questions must lie in organizing a truly national economy, one which removes the strong biases in favor of metropolitan growth and large-scale industrial enterprises which provide little employment. The key concept we shall use is that of access to a nationwide system of production, distribution, and consumption. Small farmers and businessmen need access to the means of production, the financial system, the markets, and to technical knowledge. Workers need access to remunerative employment and to suitable goods on which to spend their incomes. All these groups need access to a range of social services such as power, transport, schools, and health facilities. Only if these needs are met will the majority of the population become participating members in the national life of the society.

Access involves both physical proximity and a set of institutions that is capable of mobilizing the resources and energies of the people. With the strategies followed by dual societies, the best way to achieve physical proximity to the desired facilities is to migrate to a large city, where the investment in industry and infrastructure has been concentrated. Even when a migrant arrives, he may well find that access to modernizing institutions is restricted to privileged groups.

How then can a developing country broaden access, so that more of its citizens may become part of the society and thus join the ranks of those with adequate incomes who can consume and invest? One part of the answer lies in organizing people in institutions which create the conditions of access to the great mass of small producers—the subject of further discussion in chapters 5 and 6. Another part of the answer is a radically different concept of locating investment and infrastructure so that people may have access to these facilities where they live now. "Planning strategy in developing countries must emphasize the growth of small and intermediate regional centers, to offer market, service and storage facilities, and light labor-intensive industries processing local materials."[5] Such a strategy will provide large numbers of nonfarm jobs outside the national capital. It will also provide farmers with the necessary agricultural supplies, marketing facilities, and consumer goods needed to give them the incentive and ability to become viable commercial producers.

To expand upon the analogy of the oasis in the desert, we can visualize this alternative strategy as an interlocking series of canals and ditches of various sizes crisscrossing the entire desert. The point is to provide a hierarchy of agro-urban communities, placed strategically throughout the countryside, to link the large cities to the villages. The village itself can rarely be the starting point for innovation: it is too small and the traditional restraints on innovation are too deep-rooted. In the transition from nomadic to settled life thousands of years ago, "the remaking of man was the work of the city." More recently, the ideas of change has been institutionalized in urban centers and have emanated out into the countryside.

However, the range of influence of an urban center is limited. If, therefore, all of the rural hinterlands of a country are to benefit from the modernizing influence of the town, then the local urban center can never be very far away. This is especially true when the forms of transport used by the mass of ordinary people are still primitive, say, 2 to 3 miles per hour.

Organizing Space

A national economy requires the organization of space, the concentration of development activities in the urban centers of the different sized spatial units, a system of infrastructure within and between spaces, and the integration of agricultural and industrial development (this portion of the subject is discussed in chapter 6). Each level of urban center would contain the activities appropriate to its size. This would overcome the current gross imbalance between investment in the large cities and the rest of the country.

What types of activities need to be located in each level of a hierarchy of agro-urban centers in the early stages of development? Table 3-1 gives a simplified illustration of how space can be organized effectively. A few of the variables that need to be considered when space is being organized for the first time are also shown. If read across, table 3-1 shows the increase in size, complexity, and number of activities as the geographic area and the population are increased. If read from top to bottom, the table shows some of the important activities that need to be organized in the urban center of each area.

As stated in the previous chapter, two functions of the central government are to identify the types of activities which should be organized at each level of the national economy and to create the regional and local planning organizations needed to bring these activities into being.

The township urban center should also contain, in addition to those things shown on table 3-1, a post office and electric power. The latter is particularly important for there must be some design for rural electrification. No developing country can afford to electrify at random endless thousands of small villages, as is happening now. Electricity is used for production, in service industries, and in offices before it is used for domestic consumption. From 2/3 to 3/4 of the total demand for electricity comes from the kinds of economic facilities that need to be concentrated in rural-urban centers. The obvious way to begin rural electrification is to run secondary transmission lines to these rural-urban centers and to expand out into the countryside as rapidly as demand permits. Where irrigation requires pumping with large numbers of small pumps, this expansion can be started as soon as the urban center is connected to the national or regional grid.[6]

Table 3-1

Activities Needed at Local, District, and Regional Levels of a National Economy

	Local Level	District Level	Regional Level
Political Name of Area:	Township	County	Province or State
Size of Market Area:	Local Agricultural Market Area	Sub-Regional Market Primarily Agriculturally Related	Regional Market A Mixture of Agricultural and Non-Agricultural Activities, the Latter Usually Predominating
Size of Urban Center:	Small Market Town	Large Market Town or Small City	Intermediate-sized City or Regional Center
Transport	Single lane, low standard (probably dirt), low speed roads; roads that will link the great mass of villagers to the national market	1. Where the county is the lowest political unit, the same single lane roads listed under township. In addition, some: 2. Narrow, two-lane, simply paved, medium-speed roads suitable for at least small trucks	"Modern" high speed roads for all types of vehicles
Formal school systems	Primary school, and, as a country advances, a secondary school	Primary and secondary schools, and later, vocational training institutes in at least some of them	Primary and secondary schools and in a few that will become large regional centers, a university; also vocational and subprofessional technical institutes

Financial institutions	1. Banking section of the local farmer cooperative, primarily to mobilize personal savings and provide production credit for individual farmers 2. Depending on the population and the level of economic activity—a private bank to finance retailing and personal service businesses. Until the level of activity has risen considerably, these businesses may need to depend on a private bank in the county town.	1. The farmer cooperative at this level will provide production credit for nearby farmers but should emphasize investment in facilities—market, transport, storage, etc. 2. Private bank to provide full range of banking services 3. Perhaps also urban credit unions	1. The farmer cooperative will provide the same services as listed under township and county for nearby farmers. At least some of the province capitals should have a regional office of the national cooperative bank to provide capital to the local cooperatives 2. Private banks to provide the full range of banking services. 3. At least some of the province capitals should have a regional office of a government industrial development bank, especially for small business
Storage	Simple warehouses, fertilizer and feedgrains will require most of the space	In addition to simple warehouses, cold storage, and perhaps also humidity-controlled storage	The full range of storage and warehousing facilities

Table 3-1 (cont.)

	Local Level	District Level	Regional Level
Factories	Grain mill, oilseed mill, perhaps a feedmill. Some artisan-type businesses but perhaps no other factories	Same as township plus processing plants, small consumer goods and construction companies. Some will have building materials plants, and possibly small agricultural machine shops, such as irrigation pumps	Same as township and county plus a wide range of factories. Some provincial capitals will become regional centers of industry, marketing, transportation, education, health, and be essentially nonagricultural cities. Others will remain small and primarily dependent upon agriculturally-related activities
Health	Dispensary, initially staffed with paramedical personnel	Large clinic or small hospital with some beds. Supervision and some in-service training of township paramedics	Hospital. Some provincial capitals will become regional medical centers with medical colleges, research, and formal training of paramedical personnel and medical technicians

The Base Unit and Its Urban Center

Organizing shapeless space and large numbers of market towns is so obviously necessary in a modern economy that the reader may be surprised to be told the job is still undone. Why? Partly because space and urban centers were organized so long ago in Europe and North America, and as a result, we have almost forgotten it happened. Sometimes we are not conscious of problems long since solved. The last act in the organization of space in the United States was incorporated in the Northwest Ordinance of 1787, which prompts one to suggest that its author, Thomas Jefferson, was the first modern regional planner.

A second reason for the indifference to spatial organization is that many planners and social scientists have viewed rural development as the reconstruction of a village rather than the reconstruction of rural society.[a]

In addition to the need for outside stimuli, villages are generally too small to support the institutional base required for modernizing rural society. For example, the average size of India's 565,000 villages, as of the 1961 census, was 637 people. More than 350,000 of these villages had fewer than 500 inhabitants, which means fewer than 100 families.[7] This is too small a population base for effective local government or a farmer cooperative. Such small communities are too small to support the administrative and overhead costs of these essential institutions of local development, let alone pay the costs of needed investment.

Furthermore, the individual village does not have enough children for a school system, nor enough patients to support a doctor, nor enough nonagricultural labor for manufacturing and service industries. There are not enough consumers to support an efficient retailing system, nor is there enough economic activity to justify certain types of technology, such as trucks, or certain essential institutions, such as banks.

Some Examples

The models must, of course, be applied flexibly in adjusting to the circumstances of individual countries. Japan and Taiwan have townships that are responsible for the kind of activities shown in column 1 of table 3-1. Yugoslavia, however, does not have townships. Some of the larger communes have "sub-centers" for agriculture. Otherwise the functions shown in the township column of table 3-1 are performed by the commune (or county). At the intermediate level the functions shown in the province column are divided between the 44 district urban centers and 5 regional cities of the country.

In the small and homogeneous island of Puerto Rico, regional planning is managed from above by the Planning Board. Planning is based on regional

---

[a]As, for example, the TCD programs discussed in chapter 2 or the village cooperatives discussed in chapter 5, or most agricultural extension programs.

"socio-economic profiles" and "feasibility" studies of local resources, local markets, and the size and quality of the labor force; and also by preparation of master plans for development of rural-urban centers. Much of the detailed study is done by local governments and local groups of interested citizens. Unlike most countries where Five Year Plans are prepared by civil servants with little consultation with nongovernmental persons, Puerto Rico has emphasized private participation in public planning from the very beginning, partly to develop a mutual interest between public and private parties in the plan's success, and partly to stimulate private investment. "Planning is a device for allowing many people of moderate skills to contribute to wise decision-making, rather than leaving it wholly to the great skill of a small group of leaders."[8]

By using its statutory powers to supervise regional and local planning, the Board is able to coordinate the development of systems in all the different-sized spaces of the island economy (in transport, power, and so forth), to select the most appropriate regions or cities for certain types of investment and the most appropriate investments for each region and urban center. The whole process is supported by the industrial development program of the Economic Development Administration.[b]

This regional planning system has been combined with a series of economic incentives designed to induce new investors to build their factories outside of San Juan. Gradually, industrialization has spread throughout the island. In 1953, when *Fomento* was still emphasizing increased manufacturing without much regard to location, 60 percent of the new factory jobs were located in San Juan and only 40 percent in the rest of the Commonwealth. By 1967 the balance had been more than reversed: only 28 percent of the new jobs were in the capital; 72 percent were distributed throughout the island. During the 1970s the Planning Board of Puerto Rico hopes to increase the latter percentage to no less than 85.[9]

Leaving aside the communist countries other than Yugoslavia, there are only a handful of developing countries which have set about organizing space systematically—Puerto Rico, Taiwan, Israel, and Yugoslavia. Egypt and Korea, in this field as in many others, are well above average Third World performance, as are several African countries. In some countries there are regional areas which now have some of the distribution of functions shown on Table 3-1, not as a result of government policy but as a result of the energy of enterprising farmers and businessmen. Parts of the Punjab in northwest India is one example and some areas of southern Brazil, another. Otherwise governments have tried to extend their administrative arm down to the village level, leaving both people and space unorganized.

The organizational base in the successful countries would be called, in English, either a township or a county. Taiwan and Japan are township-based. Puerto Rico and Yugoslavia are county-based. Whatever the name, there is a good deal of variation in the average size of the local area according to population density and the topography of the land. In Taiwan the average size of a

---

[b]This agency is better known by its Spanish name, *Fomento*.

township is 45 square miles; in Japan, 120. Puerto Rico uses the word "county" to describe its local government areas. These counties, however, are about the same size as a Taiwanese township. And in Yugoslavia, the commune (county) averages 175 square miles.

The principal constraint on the size of the local area is the means of transportation. In earlier days, the United States market towns served an area with a radius up to about ten miles. Twice this distance—that is, from village to town and home again—was about the maximum distance a horse could travel in one day, allowing several hours in the town for the farmer, and sometimes his family, to do their business. In today's developing countries, the mass forms of transportation are still primitive, animals of the area or perhaps a bicycle.[c] The radial limit for a viable rural center is about the same as in the United States a century ago.

An American authority on regional planning in developing countries, E.A.J. Johnson, concludes that the optimum size of the local market area in India is 70 to 75 square miles. The radial limit of such an area is 5 or 6 miles. Since townships and counties are not, of course, perfect geometric forms, the configuration of the area, as well as its size, will determine whether subcenters will be needed to reach all farmers, as in the case of the Yugoslav commune.

On the basis of the optimum size of 70 to 75 square miles mentioned in the preceding paragraph, India needs 12 to 14,000 urban centers spread across the country. Today there are fewer than 3,000. Harking back to the population projection for Bombay and Calcutta—an increase of 92 million by the year 2000—let us assume for the moment that all of these people could be attracted to the 10,000 local urban centers which India needs. The nightmare of masses of millions in these two cities simply disappears. Instead, there would be 10,000 market towns with an average population of 9,200.

Our assumption is, of course, unrealistic; as also, hopefully, the projection for Bombay and Calcutta will turn out to be. But the contrast between the two projections dramatizes the enormous and essentially untouched potential for a reasonable distribution of urban populations among numerous urban centers that could become reality through the organization of a national economy.

Table 3-2 shows the number of villages per urban center in a few spatially organized and unorganized countries.

From table 3-2, we find some indication of the vast need for urban centers in the rural areas to allow farmers access to the facilities for commercial agriculture, to provide them with consumer goods and services, and to serve as alternatives to the big cities for migrants. Organizing space through the creation of market towns should have high priority in the policies of nearly all developing countries. Unless this is done, "modern" society will be too far away from villagers for them to become involved in development. Agricultural progress does not, in fact, begin on the farmers' field. It begins in towns where the institutions and systems are organized to link the farmer to the national economy.

[c]In Taiwan and Korea farmers use the "garden" tractor for local transport.

Table 3-2
Number of Villages per Urban Center

Spatially Organized Countries[a]	
Israel	6
France	10
Denmark	11
Great Britain	16
Spatially Unorganized Countries	
Chile	77
Argentina	86
Malaysia	87
Turkey	117
India	185
Algeria	218
Iran	269
Indonesia	355

Source: E.A.J. Johnson, *The Organization of Space in Developing Countries* (Cambridge, Mass.: Harvard University Press, 1970), p. 175.
[a]The writer has not been able to find the exact ratio for Taiwan, but it is a little less than 15 to 1.

A "progressive rural structure,"[10] involves not only an urban center with appropriate facilities but also an infrastructure to link farmers to the center and regional and national levels. Once again, the deficiency is at the local level— where most of the people live. As noted earlier, countries and aid agencies have long been investing in infrastructure at the national level. In somewhat lesser measure the same is true of the regional level. By now most provincial capitals are linked to each other and to the national capital by road or rail, or both. Most of these cities have electricity and other utilities. There is also a highway system comparable to "state roads" in the United States that links the larger towns of a province to the provincial capital. By now many of these "larger towns" also have electricity and other utilities.

Whereas the urban population has access to the regional and national transport system, many villagers do not. How many miles of farm-to-market roads a country actually needs is one of these subjects on which there has been virtually no research. Obviously, the mileage will vary with the density of population and the physical characteristics of the area.

Table 3-3 suggests that the lack of farm-to-market roads in developing countries may well be a serious problem. In Taiwan and Korea there are large numbers of dirt roads that connect villages with a modern transport network used by trucks. In the former there are 2.7 miles of farm-to-market roads per square mile of cultivated land; in the latter, 2.8. In Bangladesh during the short-lived rural

Table 3-3
Farm-to-Market Roads per Square Mile of Cultivated Land, Mid-1960s

Country	Miles[a]
Korea	2.7
Taiwan	2.6
Bangladesh	2.5
Chile	1.9
Colombia	1.6
Philippines	1.1
India	.8
Pakistan	.7
Tunisia	.6
Iran	.5

Source: *Statesman Yearbook* (London: St. Martin's Press, published annually), for road mileage; and *Production Yearbook* (Rome: Food and Agricultural Organization of the United Nations, published annually), for arable land data.

[a]In the rich countries the ratio is generally a little higher than the first three countries on the table. In the United States, France, and Japan it is about 3-1/4. The metric equivalent of this formula is approximately 1-3/4 kilometers of farm-to-market roads per square kilometer of cultivated area.

public works program in the 1960s, county and township governments connected most of the villages to the national transport network. Today there are 2.5 miles of farm-to-market roads for each square mile of cultivated land. As table 3-3 shows, road mileage in rural areas in developing countries is generally very low.[11]

The significance of these ratios is this: in the United States in the mid-1960s the amount of production inputs moved to the farm and the produce moved off the farm was 3,700 tons per square mile. This works out to one 5 ton truck every day, assuming it is loaded in both directions. In the intensive cultivation systems of Japan and Taiwan the tonnages are even higher. However, in traditional agriculture where much of the crop is consumed on the farm, the amount transported may be less than 100 tons per square mile. Such small quantities can and are carried on people's heads, or suspended on pails carried across the shoulders, or by bullock carts or "country" boat. Further, the cost of primitive transport is actually very high, perhaps 20 to 40¢ per ton mile or more,[12] as compared to 10¢ per ton mile or less for high speed trucks or other modern transport. The enormous requirement for transport in a modern agricultural system and the high cost of primitive transport are both reasons why the local market town, or at least an agricultural subcenter, cannot be very far away. Farmers can be induced to use primitive transport for the last several miles of the distribution system, but not for long distances and not for a trip that takes more than one day.

A second element of a local infrastructure system is storage. Warehouses are needed both to store production supplies and crops, of which fertilizer and food-grains are much the bulkiest. There is more involved than just the convenience of a local warehouse.

The local grain storage warehouse can be used to increase the subsistence farmer's income by giving him a share of the profits of marketing in addition to his profit from production. The subsistence farmer's marketing problem is well known. He is forced to sell his crop at harvest time when prices are lowest. Either he is in debt and harvest time is the traditional repayment time, or else he has no way of storing his crop until prices rise above the seasonal low. Traditionally, the landlord, moneylenders, and merchants own whatever storage exists and reap the benefits from price fluctuations, which tend to be much greater in the poor countries than in the rich countries.

Many countries have increased their grain storage capacity in recent years. They have not tried to use storage as a means of reorganizing the traditional marketing system, even though it is popular in many countries for politicians and the press to censure 'middlemen' for their alleged exploitation of the subsistence farmer. And some countries, such as India, have built warehouses in the city rather than in the countryside where farmers can have ready access to them.

In India, for example, in the mid-1960s, most of the storage facilities for foodgrains owned or rented by the government were located in sizeable cities. Although the warehouses are controlled by the government, most of the space was leased to private persons. Only a little more than 1/10 of the space was actually used by farmers, through their cooperatives, whereas 4/5 was leased by middlemen. The problem is that warehouses in the city are not within easy reach of the farmers, and the farmers are not organized to gather together their own production in large quantities and carry it into the city to be stored until they can reap for themselves the benefit of higher prices. These functions are still performed by the traditional middlemen. Hence, they lease the very high proportion of government storage capacity.[13]

Solving the storage problem and raising farmers' income a little can be achieved simultaneously and easily by putting farmer cooperatives into the warehouse business. In Taiwan a small warehouse was the first facility built by the farmer cooperatives when the reconstruction of the island's rural economy began in the early 1950s. However, as we shall see in chapter 5, most farmer cooperatives in the Third World do not do enough business to finance even a small warehouse, India being one example.

The foodgrain warehouse is one example of the way in which planners can and should use investment in infrastructure to influence the distribution of incomes as well as for the construction of the necessary physical facilities of a national economy.

Concerning the third element of a local infrastructure, electricity, nothing need be added to the point mentioned earlier—that a network of different sized urban communities provides the needed design for electrical transmission systems.

Thus, the lack of access to the necessary infrastructure of a modern economy is one of a number of reasons why subsistence farmers cannot become modern farmers—even if they want to.

Location of Market Towns

Granting that large numbers of market towns need to be built, where should they be located and how do governments decide the priority in which they should be located?

Not much research has been done on either question. Answering the first, locating market towns may not be difficult. Even in very backward and poverty-stricken areas, there is a marketing system functioning now. The focal points of that system are already known to the villagers and local traders. A village may be located on or near a river, or it may lie in a flat area and be more accessible than other villages. Or, a series of villages may long since have become local centers because each is a day's travel from the next. There are many such reasons which explain why some villages already have locational advantages over the others. If this local knowledge is combined with the transport and size criteria discussed earlier, then the modern market towns of the future can be identified. The problem of organizing market towns is not so much a matter of locating them through some set of theoretical criteria as of identifying and building upon the centers of local market activity that already exist.

As to priorities, economists and politicians are likely to propose different solutions. The economist will recommend using established technical criteria[d] to classify local market areas as, say, high, medium, and low potential.[14] He will then recommend that investment be concentrated in the high potential areas, for several reasons. First, presumably GNP will rise higher and faster. Secondly, if governments use tax policy wisely, they will be able to tap this increase in GNP for investment in medium and low potential areas.

The politician will argue that his constituents must share in the benefits of public investment, even if they happen to live in medium and low potential areas. Granting that high potential opportunities should be exploited, we agree with the politician. While physical and economic resources can, to some considerable extent, be identified and measured, the geographic location of human initiative and ingenuity cannot.

Enterprising local leadership can compensate for the dearth of resources. In fact on a national level, there appears to be no particular connection between resources and wealth. Some countries are rich in spite of nature's stinginess—

[d]Crops currently being produced, the existing transport system, the availability of financial institutions, and so forth.

Japan, Switzerland, Britain, Denmark. And some countries which are rich in natural resources are still poor in GNP—India, Indonesia, Brazil, and a few countries in Africa. This paradox, if paradox it be, exists within countries as well as between countries.

The Cost of a Network of Agro-Urban Communities

At first blush the cost of financing large numbers of market towns and expanding intermediate-sized cities may seem like an enormous addition to already strained development budgets. In fact, we now know from the recent history of Taiwan, Yugoslavia, Israel, and Puerto Rico that the process of organizing a national economy, once set in motion, can be essentially self-sustaining.

A large portion of the needed investments—factories, electricity and other utilities, warehouses, market and transport facilities—are profit-making ventures and therefore should pay for themselves. Governments may need to prime the pump—through such things as tax concessions, low interest loans, and other subsidies—to get the process underway. But priming the pump is precisely what governments and aid agencies should be doing. Thus, the first warehouse built by each local farmer cooperative in Taiwan in the early 1950s was subsidized. Other warehouses and other facilities now owned by the cooperatives have been financed from the profits of their business operations.

Secondly, the necessary concentration of activities in urban centers could be accelerated if governments would locate a number of rural facilities in them, facilities which are commonly included in Five Year Plans, but which are, at the present time, being scattered about the countryside haphazardly. Planners seem to understand that metropolitan areas represent a combination and, hopefully, an integration, of many modern technologies. But when they leave the big city, planners display a curious penchant for random dispersal.

Governments have been building a school in one village, a dispensary in a second. A warehouse has been built at a spot along the road because the government happens to own the land on which it is situated. The result is that much money that could have been used to transform traditional villages into market towns has been wasted. This waste can be stopped simply by adopting a location policy for public investment.

Finally, as a national economy is organized, there must be changes in tax policy and tax administration. The principal need is decentralization of tax authorities, especially on land and other property, to regional and local planning agencies. People should be more willing to pay taxes if the money is used to improve their own communities. This subject is discussed further in chapter 5.

It is possible also that the organization of a national economy will, in the long run, save money. Not much is known about the costs of building cities of different sizes. There are at least two reasons for supposing that the cost of a single very large city may be higher than the cost of distributing the same population in a number of smaller cities—the cost of land and the cost of construction tends to be higher in metropolis.[15]

In addition, large cities require relatively more sophisticated levels of technology that may increase the cost of investment per person. For example, the per capita cost of transportation may be higher in a city so large that railways are needed to carry commuters to work than in a smaller urban center in which buses or bicycles can be used for passenger traffic.

It is almost certainly true that housing costs are higher in large cities. In densely populated areas apartment buildings are relatively more necessary than in smaller cities and towns which usually have more space for horizontal expansion. There are several cheap ways of building houses that cannot be used in apartments because of their structural nature. A number of countries have organized potential home owners into a labor force to build their own houses. The so-called "core" house, which can be built in stages, is another cheap home. The core usually consists, in the first stage, of a permanent floor, frame, and roof but temporary sidewalls. As peoples' incomes rise, the sidewalls can be made permanent, the large single room can be partitioned into smaller rooms, and if designed for expansion, additional rooms can be added.

These are simple houses, to be sure, but they offer a degree of privacy, comfort, and protection which is not possible in the shacks and huts in which masses of people now live. They can be built for hundreds, not thousands, of dollars. But they are no substitute for apartments in densely populated metropolis. Apartments cost thousands of dollars per family unit in any country.[16]

Finally, certain costs of building cities can be postponed if villagers commute from their villages to the 'agro-industry' factory located in the nearby urban center of a rural area. Investment in a local bus system or bicycles might obviate the need for housing and some of the overhead costs of cities which permanent migration requires, and thereby permit relatively greater investment in other sectors during the early stages of development, as in pre-war Japan and Taiwan.

Some Evidence for Proposed Policies

If a country sets about organizing a national economy, the flood of migrants to metropolis should be slowed down because people can find productive jobs in market towns and small cities. The nonfarm population should be broadly distributed throughout the country in urban centers of different size, rather than crowded into a few congested metropolitan centers. It ought to be possible to use population censuses to demonstrate that this is, in fact, the result of applying the policies advocated in this chapter.

Unfortunately, the statistical difficulties are so great that we have been able to identify the location of the population in only a few countries. Many countries do not try to separate the farm from the nonfarm population at the local level. There is no way to distinguish between farmers who live in villages and nonfarmers who live in market towns.

In figure 3-1, the graphs for two countries—the United States and Israel—show how the organization of a national economy induces a distribution of the population in varying-sized urban centers. The graphs for Colombia and India show how the failure to organize the countryside leads to congestion in the cities.

Because of the lack of data, we have included the United States as an illustration of how market towns should expand as development gets going. During the nineteenth century the rural population of our country declined from 95 percent of the total to 60 percent. The proportion of people living in market towns and small cities rose from 5 to 18 percent and was almost half the total urban population. This rise in market town population is primarily the result of the integration of agricultural, industrial, and commercial development, which is discussed in chapter 6.

The second graph is for Israel. Israel's achievement in population distribution is remarkable because immigrants tend to settle in cities, even when they come from rural areas in their original country. Even though a million people have emigrated to Israel, the proportion of the population living in the three metropolitan areas of Tel Aviv, Jerusalem, and Haifa is slightly less today than when the country was created. The proportion of the people living in market towns and intermediate cities has increased from 20 to 35 percent.

The effect of concentrating development in a few cities is shown in the graphs for Colombia and India. In both countries the percentage of the population living in market towns and small cities has been approximately static for decades.

There is, however, one caveat to this chapter. A hierarchy of agro-urban communities can fulfill their purpose only if farmers, artisans, merchants, and small or "tiny" businessmen have access to the institutions, facilities, and services that are located in them. Before discussing how the conditions of access can be created, we must explain why the "labor force explosion" requires a pattern of investment in today's Third World that is significantly different from the pattern of investment in the nineteenth-century West.

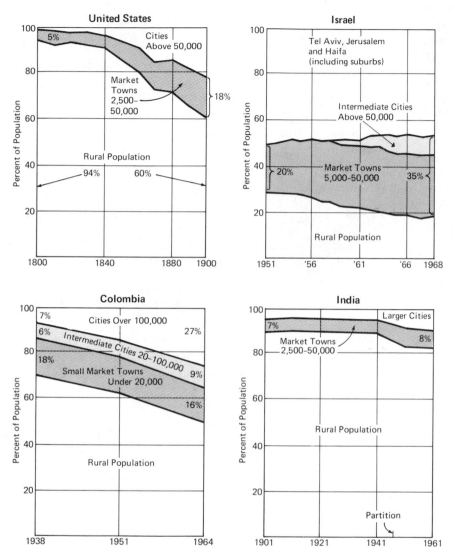

Figure 3-1. Location of the Population: United States, Israel, Colombia and India. Source: United States — *Historical Abstract of the United States* (Washington, D.C.: Department of Commerce, 1960), Series A 195-209, p. 1; Israel — *Statistical Abstract of Israel* (Jerusalem: Central Bureau of Statistics, 1949/50-1970); Colombia — Derived from ILO, *Towards Full Employment* (Geneva: 1970), p. 387; India — *Census of India* (Delhi: Government of India Press, 1901-1961).

4

The Inefficiency of Inequity

We have made several references to the growing unemployment in the poor countries, especially in their cities. The population explosion that started after the Second World War is now manifesting itself as the "labor force explosion." An unprecedented wave of workers is now entering the job market, but the number of new jobs being created is falling far short of the number of people needing them. Unless radical changes in economic organization take place, the problem of integrating marginal men into society will worsen. The president of the World Bank has described the situation graphically:

The cities are filling up and urban unemployment steadily grows. Very probably there is an equal measure of worklessness in the countryside. The poorest quarter of the population in developing lands risks being left almost entirely behind in the vast transformation of the modern technological society.[1]

One very rough estimate of the extent of unemployment in the poor countries has put the present total at 75 million;[2] that is just about the same number of people as have jobs in the United States.

The problems of defining and measuring unemployment in the poor countries are formidable. Many of the statistics are little more than informed guesses. Nevertheless, the present level of unemployment is only a partial measure of the problem. In part this is because of the dynamic of labor force growth. One rather conservative estimate has shown that in the 1970s 225 million additional workers will join the labor forces in the poor countries.[3] This means that in the course of ten years these countries must create the capital and organizational ability to provide jobs for three times as many workers as there are now in all of Britain, France, and West Germany.

In India alone, the work force may increase from 210 million in 1970 to 273 million by the end of the decade. In the first week of the 1970s, over 100,000 more new workers appeared for jobs than older workers stepped aside to make room for them; and each week, for the next ten years, the number will be higher until, in the decade's last week, the net addition of workers to the Indian economy will be about 140,000.[4]

Even this massive expansion is only one aspect of a wider employment problem—the need to provide families with the means of making a decent livelihood. The stark facts of poverty dictate that only a small proportion of the population can remain without a job for long. When people who have jobs are still living at

51

or close to the level of subsistence, there is simply no surplus to support workers without jobs. And the cushion of social security does not exist.

Because unemployment is a disaster to be avoided at all costs, people in the poor countries take whatever work they can find. Any traveller to the capital cities or the vacation areas of the poor continents is besieged by hordes of eager baggage carriers, shoe-shine boys, "money changers," and tourist "guides." Millions of workers subsist on casual labor, while others often work extremely long hours for miserable pittances. On the farms, hundreds of millions of peasants work tiny plots. While they may work very long hours during the planting and harvest seasons, they often have little to do during the rest of the year. Their resulting production bestows on their families a heritage of malnutrition and poverty. This is in part because of the nature of subsistence agriculture. But in part it is because there are now many villagers who own little land (an acre or less) or no land at all. Whether they work for themselves or larger farmers, they work primarily at the peak periods of farm work—ploughing, planting, harvesting, and threshing. At other times of the year they pick up whatever odd jobs they can find.

It is in Latin America that the combination of rapid population growth and a slow rise in the number of good jobs has had its most dramatic impact. Using the narrow Western definition of unemployment, a study by the Organization of American States estimated that the total number of unemployed in Latin America rose from 2.9 million in 1950 to 8.8 million in 1965, or from 5.6 percent of the labor force to over 11 percent. If the definition is expanded to try to encompass the unemployment and underemployment problems of the poor countries, the percentage rises. For example, the same study also tried to compare the amount of time available for work by the labor force in a year with the amount of time actually worked. It concluded that, in 1960, about 25 percent of the labor force was unemployed, or more than double the official estimate of 11 percent calculated according to Western definitions. At the same time, the labor force in Latin America continues to grow at nearly 3 percent a year.[5]

It appears that the urban population in Latin America has been growing twice as fast as the number of jobs in the cities. As an example of the results of this process, in Colombia:

At a conservative estimate, half a million Colombians, out of an active urban labor force of some 3 million, are seeking work but unable to find it. Probably as many again would like to work, but are not currently looking for it, having given up in frustration or having not even started to look with any seriousness, deterred by the knowledge that their chance of finding a job is slim. . . . In the urban areas, the shortage of work by now probably affects between a quarter and a third of the active labour force.[6]

These problems are certainly not confined to Latin America, where the population explosion had its initial impetus. Indeed, the situation of growing unemployment and underemployment seems almost endemic in the Third World. In Kenya, for example, the labor force is currently increasing by 126,000 per year. In 1969, only 27,000 new jobs were created.[7] Because of the shortage of jobs the government recently ordered employers to increase their work force by 10 percent, even though the additional workers were not needed. When Mrs. Ghandi received a large majority in India's recent election (1971), she promptly announced that her highest priority was the creation of more good jobs.

The Need for Rural Jobs

We have already seen that much of this problem is concentrated in the cities of the poor countries, where unemployment rates of 15 to 20 percent are common.[8] But as we look more closely at the various sectors where jobs must be created, the most striking fact is the size and future growth of the agricultural labor force. Indeed, whatever is done in the industrial and service sectors, it is certain that the absolute numbers of people in the rural areas of the developing countries are going to increase over at least the next generation. The need for jobs in the agricultural sector will therefore continue to grow.

We can illustrate this point by reference to India. Of the 63 million new workers predicted to enter the Indian Labor force in the next decade, 47 million are expected to need jobs in the rural areas.[9] In Latin America, if present trends continue, about one-third of the net increase in the population will have to remain in agriculture during the coming decade or two. This means that the farm work force in Latin America that has been increasing since 1950 at an average of about 500,000 per year can be expected to grow during the next fifteen years at an average of close to one million workers annually.[10]

West Pakistan has a much higher percentage of its labor force in agriculture than Latin America and is therefore more typical of the developing world. Nonagricultural employment has been rising rapidly. Yet the agricultural labor force is still predicted to grow from 7.5 million in 1961 to some 14 million in 2000.[11]

The continued growth of the number of people dependent on agriculture for their livelihood is the result of three factors: the initial large size of the agricultural sector, the high overall rate of population growth, and the relatively small capacity of nonfarm sectors to expand employment.

There is another reason to stress agricultural employment opportunities: the urgent need to slow the migration to the cities. A government that succeeds in providing more urban jobs but does nothing to improve rural living standards and employment opportunities is likely to discover that employment and unemployment in the town go hand in hand—every new job created in the city may attract two or more migrant families from the countryside.

What Has Gone Wrong?

It may seem strange that such a critical problem has gone unheeded for so long. The explanation seems to be this: Most economists and planners have thought that the needed number of jobs would be created as growth proceeds. They have had in their minds the model of nineteenth century Western industrialization. In this model, agriculture acted as a residual storage tank for the labor force, while industrial growth created enough jobs not only to absorb the increase in the labor force, but also to draw workers from agriculture into the rest of the economy. It was simply assumed that the poor countries would follow the same path; but they have been unable to.

Part of the difficulty lies in the high rates of population growth. During the period when the West European and North American countries were being transformed from agrarian to industrial societies, the labor force increased by a modest 1 percent or so every year. Nonfarm jobs were being created at 2 or 3 percent a year. There were not only enough jobs to employ the increase in the population, but farm workers were induced off the farm for town work and town life. In this century's developing countries, the population is increasing two and three times faster than in the nineteenth-century West and Japan. In order for the countries to keep up with their labor force increases, they must surpass by several times the rate of job creation achieved in Europe and North America. Only a handful of countries have succeeded in creating jobs at such a rate. The rates of economic growth in the poor countries over the past two decades have in general been considerably higher than those achieved in the nineteenth-century West. But this still has not been sufficient to create the jobs needed to employ the exploding labor force.

The other part of the problem lies in the nature of the economic development that has occurred. The emphasis on large-scale manufacturing enterprises, using sophisticated technologies, has meant that increases in production do not provide many new jobs. And each job in these industries requires a vast amount of capital; yet it is capital that is extremely scarce in the poor countries.

Take India as an example: in the period 1950 to 1964, the amount of capital used in large-scale manufacturing increased fifteen times, while the number of production workers slightly more than doubled.[12] If the concentration of capital in a few industries and on some large commercial farms continues, it is inconceivable that the growing number of potential workers will have adequate jobs by the end of the century. If, for example, 3/4 of the labor force is in agriculture and the labor force increase is 2.5 percent each year (a typical pattern in developing countries) then nonfarm jobs must be created at 10 percent each year just to employ the natural increase in the labor force. This is about double the highest rates of nonfarm job creation recorded in any country over the past two decades.[13]

Rising Concern

This situation is of grave concern not just because of the poverty that afflicts people without good jobs. The political consequences may be severe, especially as modern communications and ideologies continue to spread. It is perhaps no accident that many of these upheavals in recent history have occurred in those countries with the highest levels of unemployment. For example, in 1957, the average unemployment rate in Cuba was 16 percent, with a further fifth of the labor force reported as partially unemployed.[14] Peru and Chile are today facing similar problems. Recent troubles in the Caribbean have been blamed heavily on high rates of unemployment, especially among the young. And the devastation of the ruling party in Ceylon's general election of 1970 can be laid in part to an unemployment rate of 15 percent in the cities. This provoked Mrs. Bandaranaike, the new prime minister, to evolve an emergency employment plan as one of her first acts in office. The subsequent failure of this plan to work quickly helped to spark the insurgency in Ceylon in April 1971. The great majority of the 14,000 people detained after the insurgency was quelled were educated rural youth who were either unemployed or whose jobs did not meet their expectations.

Hence, in many poor countries, the harshness of the employment problem is helping to establish preconditions of political upheaval. The bloody attempts at revolution that are likely to follow will have serious consequences for the United States' position in the world.

At least in part because of these political considerations, the employment problem is now beginning to be recognized and a number of the aid agencies are beginning to respond. The International Labor Organization (ILO) has established a World Employment Program to focus the attention of both the numerous development assistance agencies and the developing countries on the overriding importance of the employment problem. As part of the Program, the ILO has initiated a series of country studies. The first of these to be completed, on Colombia, is a milestone in the development field.[15] The ILO proposes to reverse the planning approach that has been used almost universally for two decades: "employment becomes the target and overall growth the by-product, rather than the other way round."[16] The seeming paradox of this approach is that it will almost certainly accelerate the rate of growth even though growth is treated as a by-product. We should also note that many of the ILO proposals for increasing productive employment in Colombia are similar to the propositions being discussed in this book.

Other aid agencies are also sponsoring major research projects on the employment problem—the World Bank, the American Agency for International Development, and the Organization for Economic Cooperation and Development, successor to the organization originally set up in Western Europe to help administer the Marshall Plan.

The creation of jobs was also the major theme of the recent report on Latin American development written by the eminent Argentine economist, Raul Prebisch.[17] At about the same time, the Pearson Commission on International Development concluded that "the failure to create meaningful employment is the most tragic failure of development."[18]

What Can be Done?

If the poor countries are going to achieve development that involves the great majority of their populations, then they must create new jobs to bring people into the national economy. The labor forces of the poor countries represent vast resources of production potential which are far from fully tapped. If these workers could be put to work effectively they could add to the capacity of the economy and expand the market for goods.

But labor needs to be combined with other things to produce goods; land and capital in the case of agriculture; capital and raw materials in the case of industry. In dual societies the distribution of these complementary factors tends to be highly unequal: much of the best land is in the hands of a few large landowners, and most of the capital is tied up in a few huge modern factories and the "primary" infrastructure discussed in the preceding chapter. Because of this unequal distribution, only a small percentage of the labor force has good jobs, and these people, in a sense, form an aristocracy of labor.

Economics dictates that a country can best achieve high rates of economic growth by the fullest use of its resources. This means that most poor countries should make intensive use of their most abundant resource, labor, while husbanding carefully their scarce resources of land and capital. In practice, however, dual society countries have neglected this principle, to the detriment of broad-based development. Under political pressures from the elite groups that support them, dual society governments have encouraged large-scale, capital-intensive industries and large-farm, mechanized agriculture. Interest rates have been kept low, so that politically powerful entrepreneurs are favored with subsidized credit to build cheaply their empires in land or large industries. Foreign exchange has been overvalued so that the rich can import at artificially low prices in terms of their own domestic currencies capital goods such as tractors and steel mills, and luxury items such as air conditioners and automobiles. Wages in the modern large-scale part of the economy have been forced upward, encouraging the use of capital instead of labor. This artificial system of pricing has benefited the elites at the expense of creating new jobs and accelerating economic growth.

As one example of what has been happening, in Pakistan the domestic price of wheat during the Green Revolution has been maintained at double the world price. At the same time the larger farmers have been paying only 50¢ on the dollar for the very same tractor for which a farmer in the United States pays a dollar on the dollar.[19] With the price of tractors subsidized in this fashion, it obviously pays the large farmer to replace his farm work force with tractors. But how are the displaced workers to earn a living?

An alternative way exists to organize a labor force, bring workers into productive jobs, and spread the available land and capital among them. This route has been pursued in the modernizing societies. It involves making capital and land expensive because they are scarce, and encouraging the creation of jobs by allowing wages to be established at an appropriate level in relation to the other two factors of production. This leads to the most efficient use of the available resources for the society as a whole and consequently to the highest rates of economic growth. It also brings more people into the mainstream of society through jobs and by allowing small-scale entrepreneurs access to the means of production, the financial system, the market, and knowledge. In these ways, too, the distribution of income in, say, Korea, Taiwan and Israel, is made much more equal than in the Philippines or Mexico.

Westerners as well as Western-trained planners in the poor countries have been taught to think of small-scale, labor-intensive operations as inefficient, as a type of investment that retards economic growth. Where labor is in short supply and capital is plentiful (as in North America and Europe) then the way to increase production is, indeed, to use more machines. But where capital is scarce and labor is plentiful, then output can be raised by increasing the number of people who have a productive job. However self-evident this point may seem, it is precisely the point that has been overlooked because of the assumption that the Western pattern of development would be repeated.

In the final two sections of this chapter we shall show how modernizing societies have made full use of their labor forces. In agriculture these societies have combined large numbers of workers with small plots of land to create highly productive small-scale, labor-intensive agricultural systems. In industry they have combined large amounts of labor with small doses of the scarce resource, capital, thus creating a network of viable labor-intensive industries.

Jobs in Agriculture

Two-thirds of the people in the Third World gain their livelihood from farming. The absolute numbers of people dependent on the land is going to increase over the next generation. How can these people—one and a half billion of them—be lifted from poverty? To many Westerners, this may appear impossible. The rural areas of many of the poor countries are already very crowded in comparison to Europe or North America. For example, the average size of a farm in the Philippines is 10 acres and in India only 5.5. By comparison, the average farm in Denmark is 60 acres and in the United States 320 acres. In parts of Africa and Latin America there is more land, but the subsistence farm rarely exceeds 10 to 15 acres.[20]

By Asian standards, however, India and the Philippines are not yet all that crowded. Table 4-1 shows that Japan and Taiwan have considerably more agricultural workers per 100 acres than India, the Philippines and many other countries. Yet job creation is not a major problem in these two Asian success stories. We may therefore conclude that underemployment in agriculture in developing countries is not the result of too many people on the land. Rather, it is the result of the failure to organize the kind of small farm, labor-intensive agriculture system which exists in Japan and Taiwan, and, to a considerable extent, in Egypt and Korea. Table 4-1 also shows the number of agricultural workers per 100 acres for other countries mentioned in this book.

Can the hundreds of millions of small farms in the poor countries be made productive and efficient? The technological means for such a "minicultural" (as opposed to an agricultural) revolution exist—farmers in Taiwan and Japan are among the most productive in the world. Their yields per acre are three to six times higher than yields in the Philippines, India, and other developing countries. A minicultural revolution is primarily labor-intensive. It is also primarily chemical and biological, not mechanical. Machines and tools are used to augment human labor rather than to displace it. They are designed to provide farmers with a decent living, not drive them into the cities. "It is enormously important to create the conditions necessary for expanding farm output mainly by making available new inputs such as improved varieties, fertilizers, and other biological-

Table 4-1
Agricultural Workers per 100 acres, 1965

Country		Number of Workers Per 100 Acres
Japan		87
Taiwan		79
India		36
South Korea		79
Philippines		29
Ceylon		49
Colombia		20
Brazil		17
Mexico		12
Egypt		71
Israel		11
Yugoslavia		29
Morocco		10
United States	Less than	2

Source: Derived from tables in FAO *Production Yearbook*, 1969.

chemical forms of capital, improved implements useful for breaking seasonal bottlenecks, and improved technical knowledge inasmuch as these are complementary to the farm-supplied resources of labor and land. . . ."[21] How this can be achieved is the subject of the next chapter. In the context of mobilizing the exploding labor force, however, let us examine the question of efficiency of resource use in a minicultural system.

Until recently most experts have supposed that a subsistence farmer was not a good investment because his farm is so small. It was felt that not only could the small farmer not take advantage of economies of scale (reducing costs through large-scale operations), but also that the cost of investing in each of millions of small-holdings was higher than the gains. At the same time, it was assumed efficiency would be achieved by combining increasing quantities of machinery with decreasing numbers of workers—the traditional West European and North American way of increasing "output per worker." This concept was borrowed from our experience in which labor was the scarce resource. It has led, in dual societies, to the concentration of agricultural investment in large-scale commercial farms where big machinery is used to raise the output of each of the few remaining workers. The huge subsistence sector generally has been neglected.

However, in the developing countries where the demographic circumstances are so very different from Europe and North America, output per worker should not be the sole determinant of efficiency. "It is true that labor productivity (output per worker) is consistently higher on large farms, but this is hardly a measure relevant to policy in a labor surplus economy. Higher labor productivity on large farms is primarily related to mechanization and labor-saving technologies. . . . Land-saving technologies such as improved seed varieties, fertilizers, insecticides, improved weeding and irrigation can usually be applied equally well and efficiently on small farms. Under conditions of abundant rural labor and continuous rapid population growth (the conditions which exist in virtually every third world country) productivity per unit of land is the most relevant measure."[22]

Output per worker must, of course, rise if living standards for rural people are to rise. But at least as important is that this rise in productivity should be shared widely among the many millions of farmers in the poor countries. In the circumstances of these countries, therefore, investment should be aimed at employing productively as many people as possible with as little capital as possible. If properly organized, the result of this combination of resources is an increase in output per acre rather than an increase in the amount of land one farmer can cultivate. Thus the cost of increasing output per acre becomes the crucial factor in determining efficiency in Third World agriculture.

Extensive research carried out over the past decade shows that output per acre is generally higher on small farms than on larger farms.[23] Examples of this evidence are shown in the graphs for India, Taiwan, and Brazil (figure 4-1).

The graph for Mexico is equally interesting: it shows the cost of investment

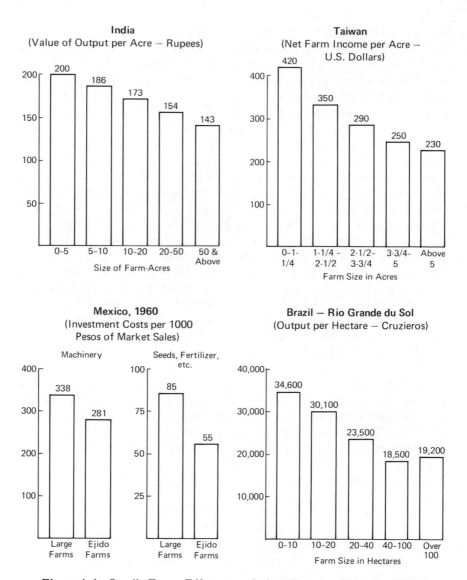

Figure 4-1. Small Farm Efficiency: India, Taiwan, Mexico, Brazil. Sources: Taiwan — Raymond P. Christensen, *Taiwan's Agricultural Development: Its Relevance for Developing Countries Today* (Washington, D.C.: Economic Research Service, U.S. Dept. of Agriculture, 1968), p. 41. India and Brazil — Lester Schmid, *Relation of Size of Farm to Productivity* (Madison, Wisc.: Land Tenure Center, University of Wisconsin). Mexico — Folke Dovring, *Land Reform in Mexico* (Washington, D.C.: AID, Spring Review of Land Reform, 1970), p. 52.

per 1,000 pesos of agricultural market sales. The cost of seeds, fertilizer, and other production inputs for the same quantity of marketable produce is 1/2 higher for large farms than for the *ejido* holdings (the Mexican name for the small farm beneficiaries of Mexico's land reform program). The difference in the cost of farm equipment and machinery is rather less, about 1/5, and is also cumulative rather than a cost for each crop. In Mexico, therefore, national income would be increased more rapidly if the available investment funds were focused on the small farm sector. Instead, Mexico has pursued the opposite path, with dire results for the welfare of the rural poor as we shall see in the next chapter. The Mexican policy has meant that the "larger private farms are using more of the hardware that might otherwise have been invested toward even more rapid industrialization of the country."[24]

If countries have an appropriate measure of efficiency in agriculture, and suitable institutions for organizing small farmers, then the small farm sector should be more productive at a lower capital cost than the large farm sector. The institutional arrangements are particularly important because there are some aspects of farming that require a certain minimum scale of operations if costs are to be reasonable. As one writer has expressed it, "For some purposes (marketing, processing, the manufacture and distribution of fertilizer, etc.) Denmark is one big farm; for others (the production process itself) it is one hundred thousand farms."[25]

One of the most difficult policy issues connected with efficiency and the minimum size of operations is the use of tractors and combines in agriculture. In Europe and North America, where labor is scarce and expensive, large machines are the obvious way of lowering costs and raising output per worker; in a word they are the most efficient mode of operation. A tractor does, however, require a considerable minimum size of farm for efficient use. This concept has been carried over to the poor countries. Planners seem to have an almost romantic fascination with large tractors, as if the science of agriculture were a problem of applying the internal combustion engine to various farm operations. "In many of the newly independent countries this neglect [of institution-building] seems to be due in part to a tendency to equate agricultural development with mechanization . . . [and make the latter] the symbol of a 'modern' agriculture. This is often accentuated by a tendency of the urban-oriented leaders in such countries to turn their backs on traditional agriculture as something 'primitive.' "[26]

If these machines really were essential for agricultural progress, then large farms would, indeed, be needed to carry the high cost of large tractors and other large machines. However, the successful Asian countries have already demonstrated that large tractors are unnecessary for rapidly rising and high levels of production. Nor can it simply be assumed that tractors are always a better way of doing a farm job, though this may be true. For example, in parts of West Pakistan certain characteristics of the soil make very deep plowing necessary. Large tractors are required because neither rototillers nor animals are strong enough to plow to a depth of 14 to 16 inches.[27] But in the absence of unusual conditions of this sort, large tractors may be no improvement over smaller machines or animals. For example, in Japan and Taiwan the same high levels of productivity can be achieved regardless of whether the land is tilled with large tractors, small rototillers, or animal-drawn implements.[28] On the other hand, in countries where tractors are subsidized, as noted earlier with regard to Pakistan, tractors are made profitable for the individual farmer, regardless of these other considerations. However, this is not the best use of a country's economic resources—in other words, it is inefficient.

Because the myth of tractor efficiency lingers on,[29] and because tradition-oriented officials "safeguard their own position by inducing collective farming."[30] joint farming has been tried in a surprisingly large number of countries quite apart from the world of communist joint, or collective, farms: India, Pakistan, Iran, Tunisia, Algeria, Uganda, Ghana, Chile, Venezuela, Colombia, Mexico, and even Taiwan in the early 1950s. Except for the Israeli kibbutz, which was inspired by unique circumstance and enthusiasm, joint farming has proven to be an expensive and inefficient solution to agricultural problems, as well as highly unpopular with peasants worldwide.[31]

In those developing countries that have made the best use of their agricultural resources through appropriate institutions and technologies, the average farmer works far harder than the typical farmer in a dual society and receives much higher returns on his work. On each rice crop, a Japanese farmer spends 180 days per hectare; his Philippine equivalent less than 100 days.[32] And the yields in Japan are nearly four times those in the Philippines. Farmers in Japan and Taiwan grow three or more crops a year, while elsewhere in Asia only a small percentage of farmers grow more than one crop a year. This naturally increases the amount of work that must be done.

The kind of machines needed in small farm, labor-intensive agriculture are those which complement human effort rather than replace it, i.e., the Japanese rather than the United States' style of farm mechanization. When, for example, a farmer can switch from one-crop to multicrop agriculture, threshing the grain from the first harvest must be finished quickly so that the second crop can be planted. A simple thresher can reduce threshing time from the traditional month or more to several days. In India the time needed to prepare the seedbed, using the traditional bullocks, can be reduced from 94 to 18 hours per acre by using a mouldboard plow and a modern harrow rather than the traditional plow and plank method.[33] The revolving weeder represents an improved "cultural practice." The back-carried sprayer reduces disease and insect damage. These are examples of the kinds of implements and machines needed for modern small farm intensive agriculture. Whether the power to use them is supplied by an engine, or an animal, or by the farmer himself, they all increase the amount of labor needed.

We might also note here that the new "miracle seeds" of wheat and rice are ideally suited to small farm, labor-intensive agriculture. Achieving their full potential (which very few farmers are doing now[a]) requires careful application of other production inputs, fertilizer and insecticides, sophisticated farming techniques, and precise water control. All of these can increase the need for labor if mechanization is based on the Japanese style of tools and equipment.

Jobs in Industry

Similar problems concerning efficiency and employment afflict industry as well as agriculture. Industry in dual societies has not provided sufficient new jobs, and because of the misuse of resources, its growth has been hampered by inefficiency. In industry, as in agriculture, the poor countries' scarcest resource is capital rather than labor or land. Hence, the most relevant measure of industrial efficiency in the Third World is not output per worker but output per dollar invested. Industrial policy should therefore be aimed at increasing production with the least amount of capital. In general terms, this means two things.

First, there are many industrial enterprises which, by their nature, tend to be labor intensive rather than capital intensive. Industrial development policy, including the price structure, should be redesigned in favor of these labor-intensive industries. As we shall see in chapter 6, labor-intensive factories (producing such things as textiles, furniture, many metal products, and building materials) happen to be the kind of factories that are needed to get industry out of metropolis and to the people.

Second, whenever there is a technological choice for a factory, the poor countries should encourage the system of production which uses the fewest machines and creates the most jobs. Technology in many industries is surprisingly flexible. Machines and labor can be combined in very different proportions. Table 4-2 illustrates this point for one category of industrial production—rubber products. It gives the investment per worker in the rubber industry of a number of Asian

Table 4-2
Investment per Worker, Rubber Products, 1965

		Amount
Philippines	1965	$2,645
Japan	1965	1,756
India	1963	1,272
Thailand	1963	1,035
Taiwan	1965	756
Korea	1966	626

Source: M.M. Mehta, *Employment Aspects of Industrialization with Special Reference to Asia and the Far East* (Bangkok: ILO, 1970), p.25.

[a]Under optimum conditions the new seeds can yield as much as 8000 pounds per acre. In the 1967-68 crop year, yields of "miracle" wheat in India averaged 2365 pounds per acre, in West Pakistan 1600 pounds. Wheat yields in Western Europe have exceeded 3000 pounds per acre for several decades. Yields from the new rice seed have been running around 2400 to 2700 pounds per acre, about half the level of Japan.

countries. In principle, one would expect the amount of machinery used in manufacturing rubber products to be highest in the most advanced of the Asian countries, Japan, followed by Taiwan and Korea, and then the other countries. The actual situation is very different. The amount of machinery used in the Philippines is higher than in Japan. It is higher in India and Thailand than in Taiwan and Korea. For Japan, Taiwan, and Korea, the amounts shown on table 4-2 can be taken as an example of how capital and labor ought to be combined according to the relative supply and cost of capital and labor. For the Philippines, India, and Thailand, the figures are an example of the overuse of capital, given the enormous number of people in search of jobs. Similar variations among countries in the degree of capital per worker in manufacturing exist in other product categories.

The proponents of traditional economic theory often argue that minimizing the use of capital in industrial production will retard economic growth because relatively cheap and simple techniques are considered to be less efficient than capital intensive techniques. Thus, it is argued that capital intensive industrialization means more output for a given amount of investment and consequently more funds will be available for new investment. This, in turn, is supposed to lead to still more output and more jobs. This premise of classical economics may well be valid for the rich countries. However, figure 4-2 suggests it may not be valid for the poor countries, at least in the early stages of development. The figure shows efficiency as measured by output per unit of capital invested in different-sized enterprises in Taiwan. The figure shows that under a reasonable

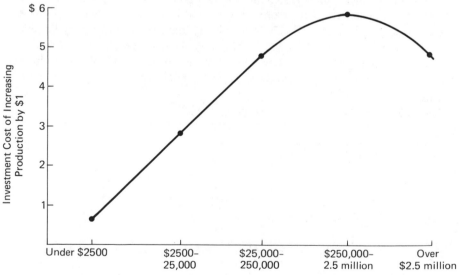

Figure 4–2. The Use of Capital in Factories, by Size — Taiwan, 1963. Source: ILO, *Development of Small Enterprises in Taiwan* (Geneva, 1967), p. 3.

price structure, small-scale factories can produce more output per additional dollar of investment than large-scale factories. This same relative efficiency in the use of capital by small firms has also been found in India, Egypt, Chile, Pakistan, Mexico, and Colombia.[34]

This same premise is also applied to personal savings and profit rates. If the argument is pushed to its logical conclusion, this means that increasing the inequality of income distribution will increase the rate of economic growth. The rich will have more personal funds to invest just as the owners of the capital intensive factories will have more profits to invest. With respect to both companies and individuals, this premise simply assumes that those who have money will, in fact, invest it.

There is now good reason to question this premise. Part of the evidence is historical, part is the result of recent research. The historical point, in much abbreviated form, is this: in the noncommunist rich countries small and geographically dispersed producers have been a part of a modern production system from the very early stages of development. They have saved and invested, increased output and created new jobs. Of Japan it is said, "It was the expansion of Japan's basic economy-agriculture and small-scale industry built on traditional functions—which accounted for most of the growth of national productivity and income during this period (1868-1914)."[35] More recently the handful of modernizing countries being cited throughout this book have created the conditions of access for small producers as well as large, for producers in market towns as well as in metropolis. To the extent that history is a valid guide to development policy, it can be said of industry, as of agriculture, that creating the conditions of access is a way of tapping the savings of an enormous number of small investors who will otherwise not invest at all.

A policy which increases the number of savers and investors is good economics. For example, new pump manufacturers in the small cities of West Pakistan have financed their shops through personal savings, selling jewelry and land, if they owned land, and borrowing from relatives and friends.[36] Such people may invest cash savings in the shares of large companies, but they do not sell jewelry or borrow money to buy shares.

There is some recent evidence which suggests that the premise of classical theory about the relationship between large firms and profit rates may not be valid, at least not in the early stages of development. First of all, some studies carried out in Japan, India, Pakistan, Philippines, Korea, Taiwan, and Egypt, in fact, suggest that the rate of profit is not always higher in large industries than small ones.[37] Table 4-3's statistics from Taiwan are almost the other way around. Not much is known about whether the owners of small factories reinvest more or less of their profits than the owners of large factories, though how entrepreneurs use their profits is obviously as important as profit rates.

Secondly, there is now reason to believe that some measure of equality in income distribution, far from slowing down the rate of economic growth, ac-

Table 4-3
Rate of Profit in Industries by Size—Taiwan, 1960

Size of Industry (By Amount of Investment U.S.$)	Profit Rate %
Less than $2,500	5.11
$2,500 to $25,000	5.61
$25,000 to $250,000	5.54
$250,000 to $2.5 million	3.04
More than $2.5 million	1.69

Source: S.C. Hsieh and T.H. Lee, *Agricultural Development and Its Contributions to Economic Growth in Taiwan* (Taipei: Joint Commission on Rural Reconstruction, 1966), p. 97.

celerates it.[38] Politicians who have long thought that increasing participation in development ought to increase the rate of economic growth will not be surprised to hear this. There are two points involved, both almost self-evident. Many of the poor are small producers—farmers or businessmen. By investing in themselves they cannot only improve their own lot in life, but they raise their country's total investment as well. The second point is that as the incomes of the poor rise it becomes possible to build a mass market, based primarily on labor-intensive goods (discussed further in chapter 6).

Third, personal savings among the rich may not be as high as classical economic theory suggests. When the mass demand for new products is low, thus limiting the opportunities for profitable investment, the rich may either spend their money on consumer goods and land or transfer their savings abroad rather than invest it in productive ventures at home. In Colombia, for example, the annual personal savings rate (exclusive of business savings) is estimated to be a mere 2 percent of national income (1961-67).[39] Personal savings should be at least three or four times higher if there is to be enough money for needed new investments.

Using Resources More Efficiently

To summarize the importance of countries making the full use of resources, and especially of their labor forces, we can examine the results of different types of policies on overall economic growth and employment. The modernizing countries have generally pursued policies which involve their work forces as fully as possible in the development process. They have made capital more expensive by raising interest rates, maintaining realistic exchange rates, and so forth.

Investors have therefore minimized the use of machines and maximized the use of workers. The modernizing countries have also involved small farmers and other small entrepreneurs in a modern production system. As a result, these countries have achieved high rates of economic growth, more efficient use of capital and land, more jobs, and a more equitable distribution of income.

With regard to the use of capital, table 4-4 gives the amount of new investment needed to increase production annually by one dollar (which economists call the incremental capital/output ratio) for a number of countries over the 1960s. Generally speaking, the investment costs of increasing production in the developing countries should be low, partly because of the shortage of capital and partly because the kind of technology needed to put people to work is relatively simple and cheap. In the rich countries, however, the investment costs of increasing production are necessarily much higher because of the high cost of sophisticated technology.

Thus, one would expect the investment cost of increasing production by a given amount to be lowest in the poor countries, such as Korea and Taiwan, somewhat higher in the almost rich, as in Israel and Japan, and highest in the most developed countries. As table 4-4 shows, however, the actual situation is very different in many of the poor countries.

The investment cost of increasing production is lower in Israel and Japan than in Latin American countries although both per capita incomes and the technological level are higher in the first two!

Table 4-4
Investment Cost of Increasing Production by $1, 1960-69

Korea	$1.70	Israel	$2.90
Taiwan	2.10	Japan	2.90
Uganda	2.40		
Brazil	$2.80	United States	$3.70a
Mexico	3.10	France	4.00
Morocco	3.20	Canada	4.10
Philippines	3.50	Denmark	4.50
India	3.90	Netherlands	5.00
Peru	4.00	West Germany	5.40
Chile	4.00		
Colombia	4.30		
Venezuela	4.90		
Argentina	5.60		

Source: U.S. Agency for International Development, 1970, Washington, D.C., and Organization for Economic Cooperation and Development, Paris, 1971.

aThe true figure for the United States is actually a little higher than $3.70. However, the total investment cost of increasing production cannot be calculated because the United States does not include government investment in the total investment figures in the national income accounts.

In India and the Latin American countries (except Brazil and Mexico) the cost of increasing production is as much as in the United States and other Western countries!

The significance of these figures may be somewhat clearer for those not accustomed to using the formulas of economics by rearranging the standard economics formula to show how much production is increased for each dollar invested.

Per capita income in Israel now exceeds $1,500, as high as in some West European countries. At this relatively high stage of development, and with the labor force almost fully employed, production increases generally require more complex and more expensive machines. Hence, for each dollar invested by Israel, one would expect the increase in production to be less than in countries where incomes are much lower and masses of people are unemployed and underemployed. Table 4-5 shows, in the first grouping, that per capita income in Israel is considerably higher than in most Latin American countries. In this circumstance one would expect the increase in production per dollar invested to be higher in the Latin countries than in Israel. Instead, it is higher in Israel!

The second grouping shows the enormous variation in the efficiency with which capital is being used in four Asian countries at lower income levels. Here one would expect the increase in production per dollar invested to be lower in Taiwan and Korea than in India, instead of the reverse. One would expect the increase in Korea and the Philippines to be about the same rather than no less than twice as high in the former. This relative efficiency in the use of capital by

Table 4-5
Average Annual Production Increase per $1 Invested, 1960-1969

Group I	Annual Increase in Production	GNP Per Capita 1969
Israel	$.34	$1570
Mexico	.32	580
Peru	.25	330
Chile	.25	510
Venezuela	.20	1000
Argentina	.18	1060
Group II		
India	.26	110
Philippines	.29	210
Taiwan	.48	300
Korea	.59	210

Source: U.S. Agency for International Development, Washington, D.C., 1970 and World Bank, Washington, D.C., 1971.

Taiwan and Korea is one way of explaining why economic growth rates in these two countries are among the highest in the world. It is also a way of explaining why per capita GNP doubled in Korea during the 1960s (an annual growth rate of 6.4 percent) whereas per capita GNP in the Philippines and India increased by less than one quarter during the same period (annual growth rates of 1.9 and 1.1 percent, respectively).

For comparison, we would note that the same figure for Japan is 34¢; and, in the most machine-oriented economy in the world, the United States, the amount is about the same as in India—26¢!

These calculations make it abundantly clear that the modernizing countries have used their limited investment funds far more effectively than have dual societies in all parts of the world.

Jobs—One Country's Experience

Turning to jobs, Taiwan is the best current example of how widespread unemployment and underemployment can be avoided by following the policies discussed in this chapter. In 1950 agricultural employment was 1.7 million.[b] It has increased at 1.2 percent a year, reaching 2.1 million in 1968. In addition, by also pursuing the job-creating market town and agro-industry policies discussed in chapter 3, Taiwan has created nonfarm jobs at the rate of more than 4 percent every year.

Averages are useful but they disguise important details. In Taiwan in the early 1950s, the job creation rate was lower than the twenty year average and only about equal to the population increases. As the momentum of development increased, the job creation rate rose. By the late 1960s it was 6 percent a year. By that time the population increase had declined to 2 percent a year, only a third of the job rate increase, because personal incentives for limitation of family size are inherent in Taiwan's development strategy (see chapter 8).

To illustrate the enormous difference in the employment potential of extensive and intensive agriculture, let us suppose that Taiwanese agriculture were abruptly transformed into United States style agriculture, with highly mechanized, large farms and few farmers. Taiwan would need fewer than 50,000 farmers. Unemployment would rise by more than 1.5 million and from the current low level of 3 to 40 percent of the entire labor force, even though Taiwan has had one of the highest rates of job creation ever recorded! It is this capacity of small farm, labor-intensive agriculture to create jobs that is being increasingly recognized as the beginning of the solution of the employment problem. "The main burden of absorbing the increase in the labor force falls inevitably on agriculture. . . . Only a fraction of the new workers can find employment in nonagricultural sectors even if these expand very rapidly."[40]

---

[b]Including forestry and fishing, which are, however, a small part of the total.

It is true that in the long run farmers can continue to share in the general prosperity of a country only if fewer farmers cultivate more land. Even with the most efficient farming possible, the maximum income that can be earned on a one or two acre farm is clearly limited. At some point the agricultural labor force must begin to decline and average farm size must rise. At that point those who continue to cultivate the land will begin to buy the kind of agricultural machinery with which we are familiar—that which replaces labor.

Taiwan reached this point in the late 1960s.[c] The shift from farm to factory which North Americans and Europeans associate with agricultural progress is beginning, though it will, perforce, proceed more slowly in Taiwan than it did in the West because of the island country's very high population density. The point, however, is that Taiwan reached this position *after* the traditional dual economy had been transformed into a single modern economy with very large numbers of small producers and small investors; *after* the incomes of these small farmers, artisans, merchants, and others had increased several times.

The increase in the efficiency and productivity of small units is necessary, not only to achieve a more equal distribution of family incomes but also to accelerate growth and maintain it at a high level. The key to sustained rapid growth and full employment in the decades of the labor-force explosion lies in the technological advance of small units of production, first in agriculture, then in manufacturing and other sectors.[41]

---

[c]Japan first reached the same point in the 1930s and, following the dislocation of World War II, reached it again in the 1950s. South Korea appears to be very close to this point.

5

A Policy for
Developing Farmers

In one form or another most of the less developed countries face a basic issue of agricultural development strategy that can be crudely defined as a choice between the 'Japanese model' and the 'Mexican model.' ... In essence, the contrast between the Japanese and Mexican approaches to agricultural development lies in the fact that the increase in farm output and productivity in Japan resulted from the widespread adoption of improved techniques by the *great majority of the nation's farmers*, whereas in Mexico a major part of the impressive increases in agricultural output in the postwar period have been the result of extremely large increases in production by a *very small number* of large-scale, highly commercial farm operators.[1]

The dilemma of agricultural policy today in the dual society countries is that governments must rely on the larger farmers if production is to be increased quickly, particularly to feed rapidly growing populations. It is the larger farmers who already have access to the market, and credit, to production inputs and technical information; above all, perhaps they are the farmers who can be reached by the government. Small farmers, however, cannot respond to changes in government policy if they lack access to the different elements of a modern agricultural system. Furthermore, there is a strong belief on the part of governments and development assistance agencies that the way to achieve agricultural development is to follow the pattern of Europe and North America, namely, drawing the "inefficient" small farmers out of agriculture.

To illustrate: In late 1965 India adopted a short-term, production campaign type of food policy. The purpose was to increase foodgrains production from a 'traditional normal' of 90 million tons per year to 125 million tons in the early 1970s. The target was to be achieved by using "miracle" seeds,[a] concentrating fertilizer and other production inputs in the irrigated areas (which comprise only 23 percent of India's cultivated land), and price incentives to producers.[2] Similar policies were adopted in West Pakistan with respect to wheat and in the Philippines for rice. The result has been increases in production which are very likely the most abrupt and the largest in all of history. In just one year both Pakistan and India increased wheat production by no less than 40 percent and are now virtually self-sufficient in this foodgrain. The Philippines increased rice production by one-sixth in just one year and has become self-sufficient.

[a]This is the name sometimes given to the high yielding Mexican wheat seed and the IR-8 (and other numbers) rice seed developed in the Philippines. The phrase "Green Revolution" is sometimes used to describe the phenomenal increases in production in Mexico, India, the Philippines and a few other countries which the "miracle" seeds helped make possible.

However, the Green Revolution has widened the distance between large and small farmers, between landlords and tenants, between the government and the governed. In India large farmers have not been increasing but multiplying their incomes, in some instances by as much as six times, while the situation of many small farmers is essentially unchanged.[3] In all three countries some tenants and landless agricultural laborers are being displaced by United States style farm machinery which large farmers are now buying.[4] The Green Revolution is yet another example of our fondness for technical solutions to human problems. Improved seeds cannot solve the problem of unimproved farmers.

Agricultural development is first of all a human problem, not a technical problem. If all farmers have access to production inputs, the financial system, the market and agricultural knowledge, then they can improve the state of agriculture. But most farmers lack access to a modern system and thus lack both the resources and the incentives to modernize their production methods.

Giving all farmers access is essentially a problem of "institutional development," that is, creating the array of institutions in which the different elements of a modern agricultural system are organized and managed and in which a more equitable set of relationships among different groups of people can gradually evolve. The principal beneficiary of these institutions ought to be the world's countless millions of small subsistence farmers, those who cultivate ten or five, sometimes as little as just one acre of land, and who are about 3/5 of the total population of the Third World. However, most of the institutions which exist in the developing countries today are managed in such a way that few subsistence farmers have access to them.

For example, unequal access to the market is one of the reasons why the Green Revolution in India has benefitted mostly the large farmers. "The cooperative marketing societies do not have any purchasing agents in the village at all. Cultivators wishing to use their services must arrange their own transport to the market town. Worse still, the majority of marketing societies lack funds to make outright purchases of foodgrains from cultivators or even to offer substantial advances against anticipated sales proceeds. They generally act only as commission agents, arranging for sale of members' produce by open bid in the market town. This may be of some help to large landholders, but not to medium and small cultivators."[5]

Foodgrain productivity can be taken as a rough measure of: (1) the capacity of a rural society to adjust to technological change, and (2) whether all or just some of the farmers are reaping the benefits of change. In traditional agriculture foodgrains are quite literally the difference between life and death. They make up 60 or 70, sometimes even 80 percent of the diet. If the harvest is poor, the subsistence farmer does not assume he will be able to buy other foods for he does not have the money (and countries do not have the distribution systems). Rather, he assumes he and his family will go hungry. Because of the overwhelming importance of foodgrains in subsistence agriculture, in some languages people do not say, "Have you eaten?" Rather, people say "Have you had rice?" (or wheat or corn or whatever is the staple food of the area).

In the crowded countries agricultural progress on small farms should begin with an increase in the yields per acre of foodgrains, as in Japan, Taiwan, Korea, and Egypt. When the farmer understands he can grow as much foodgrain as he needs on less land, then he will be willing to use the rest of his land for other crops which he can either consume or sell (the diversification and commercialization of agricultural production).

The only countries with relatively high yields per acre and with rapid increases in yields per acre during the past twenty years are those countries in which more or less all farmers have access to a modern agricultural system—Taiwan, Korea, Egypt, Yugoslavia (see table 5-1). In a country such as Mexico, most of the increase shown on the table has been achieved by large farmers growing wheat on irrigated lands (wheat yields in Mexico exceed 2000 pounds per acre and are higher than in the United States). However, yields of corn (the small farmers' foodgrain) are relatively much lower and have risen less during the past two decades.

In the dual economy countries national averages of foodgrain productivity are not particularly high because of the drag of the relatively static subsistence

Table 5-1
Yields per Acre for Foodgrains, 1948-50 to 1968-70 (Pounds per Acre)

Modernizing Countries	1948-50	1968-70	Increase	Comparative Countries	1948-50	1968-70	Increase
Taiwan	1800	3510	1710	Japan	2920	4585	1665
Egypt	2120	3370	1250	Denmark	2670	3860	1190
Korea	1640	2850	1210	Great Britain	2155	3170	1015
Yugoslavia	1145	2185	1040	U.S.	1495	2895	1400
Dual Society Countries							
Thailand	1190	1670	480				
Chile	1125	1630	505				
Indonesia	1240	1530	290				
Colombia	915	1480	565				
Mexico	700	1265	565				
Brazil	1170	1225	55				
Philippines	930	1145	215				
Turkey	835	1105	270				
India	640	945	305				
Iran	900	950	50				

Source: Derived from tables in the FAO *Production Yearbook*, 1969, Rome, 1970 and World Crop Statistics, FAO, Rome, 1966.

sector. The same is true of fertilizer usage per acre. Granting that the "natural" fertility of the land varies a great deal according to the climate and the soil, there is no technical justification for the extremely low productivity in many of the countries shown on table 5-1. For example, Japan's volcanic soil is poor rice land. Yet rice yields in Japan are higher than in any country in which rice is the major foodgrain. The history of rice farming in Japan is one example of man's conquest of a sometimes unkind nature. "Food shortages are not due to a lack of technology, but to the inability to apply existing knowledge."[6]

To get a glimpse of the possible future of dual society countries we can look, in retrospect, at Mexico:

The great mass of the peasantry continues to work its tiny subsistence holdings with traditional backward methods. . . . The production of Mexico's two basic food crops, corn and beans, has managed to keep up with the rapid population growth in the past twenty years, but the margin of security has been slight and in drought years Mexico has been forced to spend its precious dollars to import huge quantities of corn to feed its people.[7]

Between 1950 and 1960, 80 percent of the increase in agricultural production in Mexico came from only 3 percent of the farms. The number of landless rural laborers increased from 2.3 million to 3.3 million. Because of the labor-displacing style of mechanization, the number of days worked by each laborer declined by virtually one-half, from 194 to 100. The extremely low incomes of these workers actually declined from $68 to $56 per year during the decade at the same time that per capita income for Mexico as a whole increased from $308 to $405.[8]

The prospect for India and many developing countries is a further widening of the gap between the privileged and nonprivileged groups, as in Mexico. Further, if Mexico can be taken as a guide, the population explosion will continue unabated (see chapter 8).

A dual society in agriculture can be avoided if governments are willing to give small farmers access to all the elements of an agricultural system on more or less equal terms with the larger farmers. Creating the conditions of access is not only wise social policy; as explained in the preceding chapter, it is the best economics as well.

The two principal elements of access in the crowded and exploding labor force countries are the organization of small farmers in a labor-intensive system of agriculture and reasonable land tenure arrangements. Both are required to bring the mass of small farmers into the mainstream of a country's economy.

Organizing Farmers

Leaving aside nonbusiness organizations of rural development (of which the paramount one is local government), and also the socialist collective farm, four major systems of organizing small farmers have been used in those areas of the Third World where traditional agriculture is being modernized successfully. They are:

1. Plantation agriculture embracing a very large area, often thousands of acres, worked by a wage labor force.
2. Centralized management, usually by the government, of large numbers of small freeholders, usually producing an export crop, such as the Kenya Tea Development Authority.
3. Agro-industry processing plants (a sugar mill, a textile mill, etc.) contracting with individual producers for the crops used in the factory.
4. The multipurpose[b] farmer cooperative which provides production inputs, finances, marketing, and knowledge for its members—the Japanese model.

There are, of course, a number of variations on these general types as they have been adapted to diverse local conditions. There has also been a good deal of variation in the time needed to organize both farmers and a more efficient agricultural system in accordance with levels of literacy and education, the organizational talent and experience of rural people, the extent of market development, and so forth.

All of these four ways of organizing farmers may be found in modern agricultural systems. However, the limitations of the first three methods suggest that the fourth or cooperative method is far and away the most meaningful in serving small farmers. The first three are usually single-crop organizations, whereas modern agriculture must be both diversified and capable of responding to changes in taste and market conditions. They also are tied almost exclusively to the export market. Further, in the first three, most decisions are made for—not by—the individual farmer. There may be an increase in income but these systems limit the development of a self-reliant spirit.

The argument that plantation and central management systems are justified because certain crops such as sugar, tea, coffee, rubber, and others require large-scale management and cultivation, may be part of the mythology of large farms, conventional wisdom to the contrary. In Taiwan, for example, sugar cane productivity is as high on individual small farms as on the plantations of the state-owned Taiwan Sugar Corporation. The efficiency of plantations, as compared to well-organized small farms, needs to be reexamined, especially by those who cherish the social values of a system of family farms. Planners should be mindful that efficient modern agriculture can be organized around family-owned and operated production units.

It is worth noting that thus far no small-farm country has created a modern agriculture based on the first three types—plantation, central management, or

---

[b]By multipurpose is meant a cooperative that provides access to the financial system, production inputs, the market, and technical knowledge. The multipurpose cooperatives of Japan and Taiwan have an operating division for each of these major functions.

contract farming. Rather, the principal organization used to involve small farmers in a flexible system, capable of responding to both domestic and export markets, and giving the farmer some control over his own destiny, has been the multipurpose farmer cooperative.

Organizing a nationwide system of cooperatives may seem to be a tedious and time-consuming process. Those who are anxious to increase production quickly sometimes argue that organizing takes too much time; it seems to postpone the increase in GNP that planners strive for. Uganda, for example, adopted a plan to organize between 1965 and 1975 a nationwide system of local cooperatives with regional and national federations. The reasons for this drawn-out schedule are found in the fundamental characteristics of the state of underdevelopment—lack of trained people, lack of experience at all levels, lack of capital, lack of market development, and so on. Implementation of the plan is already somewhat behind schedule. Is it worthwhile to take so many years modernizing the institutional structure of subsistence societies?

Throughout this book we shall continue to compare the historical performance of the modernizing and the dual society countries. If history is a valid guide, then organizing the people for development, even if it takes many years, is nevertheless the fastest way of achieving both rapid economic growth and a relatively stable, modern society.

Multipurpose Farmer Cooperatives

Multipurpose farmer cooperatives have an almost universal image as a business institution through which small producers can improve their lot in life and protect themselves from exploitation.

To this view, born in Europe and North America, the developing countries have added an image of the cooperative as an institutional bridge between the low productivity world of subsistence agriculture and the high productivity world of modern agriculture.

In a few countries the cooperative has turned out to be an effective bridge. Japan, Israel and Taiwan are outstanding examples of how the cooperative can involve millions of small farmers in modern agriculture. Egypt and Korea also have reasonably effective cooperatives. In these countries agricultural productivity is high and rural incomes are rising. More recently, Ceylon, Uganda, and Comilla County have initiated cooperative programs that appear to have the beginnings of success.

Elsewhere, which includes most of the developing countries, farmer cooperatives have not performed well: They have been stifled by an excess of government paternalism and control from above. When local cooperatives are organized and run by government officers, illiterate small-scale farmers usually regard them as government agencies whose purpose is to give them help in time of need.

Accordingly, many see no reason to pay their bills or repay loans. In many places, local elites have taken control of local cooperatives and operated them for their own benefit rather than the benefit of all farmer members. Part of the problem can be explained by the failure to adapt cooperative development to a social situation which is very different from nineteenth-century Europe and North America or Japan in the early part of this century.

In Europe, North America, and, to some extent in Japan, there was a long period of agricultural progress before the cooperative became important. For example, there were private banks in most county seats in the United States long before cooperatives were organized. The same was true of market towns in Western Europe and also Japan. These banks did not provide as much credit as farmers needed, nor were all farmers able to qualify for loans, but the banks constituted one essential element, at the local level, of an agricultural financing system. The cooperative came later as a second financial institution.

In the developing countries, however, private banks are still virtually unknown in the countryside. Static rural areas that have not yet been brought into the money economy do not provide enough business to justify a private bank. In such a situation the cooperative becomes more than just a low-cost source of credit. It can be the beginning of a modern financial system for small farmers.

In North America and Europe, cooperatives are viewed as business institutions through which farmers receive added economic benefits, because as members of a group they possess bargaining power which they lack as individuals. Thus, a farmer may have a somewhat higher income as a member of a cooperative than if he buys his production inputs from or sells his produce to a private merchant. By preventing the price of fertilizer from rising at the time of peak demand, or the price of produce from falling at the point of peak supply, cooperatives can help stabilize the price structure for the benefit of farmers. These are, in fact, the long established reasons for organizing cooperatives in Europe and North America.

However, in the developing countries, there are additional and even more important reasons for organizing farmer cooperatives: (1) the cooperative technique of organizing people can be used to give small farmers institutional access to the means of production, the financial system, the market, and agricultural knowledge; (2) the cooperative technique of organizing a business is itself a way of organizing many of the related elements of a modern agricultural system. Cooperatives cannot function effectively without warehousing, marketing, processing, transportation, extension, and many related functions.

Table 5-2 explains this point more fully. The left-hand column of the table lists the elements of a modern agricultural system. The right-hand column lists the possible ways by which the multipurpose farmer cooperative can improve the agricultural system of a country. The right-hand column is based on the activities of cooperatives in those countries which are cited in this chapter as successful examples of small farm, labor-intensive agriculture, the type of farming which is the most common in the Third World.

Table 5-2

Role of Multipurpose Farmer Cooperatives in Agricultural Development

Essential Elements of a Modern Agricultural System[a]	Role of Farmer Cooperatives
Research	None directly. However, the results of local verification trials (see below) are part of the data base of scientists
Farm supplies & equipment	
Seeds	Minor or major supplier
Chemicals–fertilizer Pesticides, etc.	Major supplier
Equipment, tools, and machinery	Minor or major supplier
"Progressive Rural Structure"	
Market towns	Major–by developing market, storage, and processing facilities, and a financial institution
Rural roads	None
Local verification trials	Minor–can be part of the organization and communications system between extension agents and farmers which is needed for large numbers of LVT trials
Extension service	Cooperatives can employ extension agents. Or, if the agents are government employees, the cooperative can be the organization through which farmers are reached
Savings and credit	Major– Mobilizing the savings of individual farmers to help build capital for: Providing individual production and other loans (for fixed agricultural investment or personal use) Investing, as a business-organization, in market, storage, and processing facilities
Economic incentives and government policy	Representing the interests of farmers with government agencies and politicians
Land Improvement	Operation and maintenance of government-built irrigation systems at farm level is commonly handled by a Local Irrigation District, which has many similarities to a cooperative

Table 5-2 (cont.)

Communication system	A major element of a communications system between government and farmers and between the market and the farmer

aThese are based on Arthur T. Mosher's *Getting Agriculture Moving* (New York: Agricultural Development Council, 1966) and *Creating a Progressive Rural Structure* (New York: Agricultural Development Council, 1969). Dr. Mosher, the President of The Agricultural Development Council in New York, is a recognized authority on agricultural problems in the poor countries.

This evaluation of the role of multipurpose farmer cooperatives is based on the history of small farmers in developing countries over the past several decades. The three countries which have involved all of their farmers and have achieved the most agricultural progress in this century are Japan, Israel, and Taiwan. These countries also have the most effective cooperatives.

Countries well above the average of developing countries in small farm productivity, and with reasonably effective cooperatives are Egypt and Korea. Uganda and Ceylon are beginning to be successful in using the cooperative as an institutional bridge between subsistence and modern agriculture.

There are also numerous instances of local cooperatives being the bright spots in otherwise dreary national agricultural pictures. India is one country in which certain marketing federations are doing well. In Comilla County, agricultural productivity among the cooperative members is double the country-wide average and rising more rapidly. The same can be said about individual local cooperatives in Southern Brazil and Venezuela, the Philippines and Thailand, Tanzania and Kenya, and some other countries.

In the successful countries, or local areas within certain countries, cooperatives have been used to solve precisely those problems of access for the small farmer which still remain unsolved in so much of the developing world—access to production inputs, the financial system, the market, and knowledge. Personal incomes have risen accordingly as the cooperatives have grown.

On the other hand, there are no developing countries in post-World War II experience whose small farmers are doing well without viable cooperatives.

Thus, there is much in recent history to support the notion that farmer cooperatives should be a major business institution of rural development, especially in small-farm countries.

The Social Situation of Farmer Cooperatives

If farmer cooperatives are so avowedly an instrument of progress, why have many developing countries not advanced in the manner of Japan and Taiwan or

cAs of the time of writing, the future of the Comilla project is uncertain because of the current political difficulties in Pakistan.

of Egypt and Korea? In much of the developing world the history of farmer cooperatives begins decades before development became an imperative of our time following World War II. Yet, in many countries the mass of small farmers still lacks access to a modern agricultural system.

But, as the earlier reference to the market situation in India suggests, cooperatives do not always give farmers access to the different elements of an agricultural system. What then has gone wrong in the many countries where the situation is similar?

Broadly speaking, either governments or traditional local elites, or both, have prevented cooperatives from achieving their intended purpose. "Cooperatives become forms of official tutelage, useful as temporary expedients, but tending to perpetuate official control and keeping peasants as second-class citizens."[9]

"The present study [of farmer Cooperatives in Colombia done by the United Nations] tends to illustrate how in underdeveloped societies certain institutions undergo a process of re-adaptation to the milieu which puts their functioning in a state of contradiction to their ideological objectives and doctrines. Such institutions adapt themselves to the context in which they function with the effect that, far from producing necessary changes therein, they reinforce the established social order instead."[10] Far from being a way of improving the existing agricultural system, the cooperative is subverted and made a part of the existing system by those who control it.

The manner in which local cooperatives have been organized is another illustration of the difference between modernizing and dual society governments.

In the dual societies the common pattern is for a civil servant to ask the farmers to agree to organize a cooperative society in each individual village. The president is invariably either a person of status in the local community or an individual who serves as his agent.

For the most part, whatever activities are undertaken by this type of village society are initiated by the government. Loans can be extended to members when the government appropriates funds for agricultural credit. Fertilizer becomes available locally when delivered by the government. Crops are marketed if and when the government makes the necessary arrangements. Most of whatever planning is done is initiated by the government and the mass of small farmers are not much involved. In such a system the local officers are merely intermediaries, a communications channel between remote government officials and the people.

The officers of the village society help the government officials administer whatever programs the government sponsors. Since governments are too often lax in imposing standards which assure equal treatment of all members, it becomes relatively easy for the local leaders to monopolize the benefits. In one case, "a number of small loans went for immediate consumption or for handling calamaties," a kind of poor relief program rather than a way of increasing production and personal incomes. In this same cooperative, moreover, most of the production credit funds were allocated to the larger farmers.[11]

Sometimes the leaders of a village cooperative may refuse to approve loans for small farmers on the grounds that they cannot provide adequate security. Since small free-holders generally have little security except for their land or their houses, and because tenants and sharecroppers cannot, of course, mortgage land they do not own, they lack access to modern financial systems. For such reasons as this only about half the farmers in India who belong to cooperatives, or only a fourth of the farmers in the country, are able to qualify for loans from their village societies. This type of cooperative tends to increase the gap between rich and poor rather than providing a way to involve the poor in a modern agricultural system, as we shall see further on.

This type of local cooperative—unfortunately, the most common type in developing countries—contravenes virtually every principle of a successful cooperative business.

Modernizing governments help the farmers themselves establish viable and relatively autonomous units at the level of the county or township, not the village, and federates them in regional or national associations of local cooperatives.

The government works with the local cooperative officials and relies on these officials to work with the farmer members. The government's principal function is to set and enforce minimum standards of performance so that all farmers have access to the means of production, the financial system, the market, and agricultural knowledge. When a government is seriously trying to help small farmers, it does not permit credit to be used as a relief dole for the poor and higher production for the rich.

The government's role is to help small free-holders, tenants, and sharecroppers have access to the modern agricultural system and to protect them from traditional forms of exploitation. This suggests a role of government which runs counter to the principles of cooperatives in free societies. To say this may disturb Western cooperative theorists who want cooperatives to be relatively free of government control in the European and North American tradition.

Where cooperatives have been effective—Japan, Taiwan, Korea, Egypt—the government itself has intervened on behalf of small farmers and created and sustained the conditions of access for all. Thus, the question over the role of government in developing countries is not whether the government should be involved, but rather, how the government is involved, and whether the government is willing to withdraw gradually as the conditions of access are created and farmers learn how to manage their own cooperative business enterprises. Hence, the long-run role of governments might be described as beginning as champion, continuing as partner, and abiding as friend.

Table 5-3 shows how the modernizing and dual society ways of organizing farmer cooperatives have affected the mass of small farmers. The table shows the proportion of farmers belonging to cooperatives. In the modernizing countries the proportion of farmers who belong to a cooperative is very high. In sharp

Table 5-3
Percentage of Farmers Belonging to Cooperatives, Late 1960s

Country	Percentage	Recent Trends in Membership
Modernizing		
Japan	Virtually 100	–
Taiwan	Virtually 100	–
Korea	Virtually 100	–
Ceylon	80	Rising slowly
Comilla County, Bangladesh	60	Rising slowly
Uganda	50	Rising 8% per year
Dual Society		
India	50	Rising slowly
Brazil	28	Rising in South, Declining in Northeast
Chile	28	Rising slowly
Philippines	17	Rising slowly
South Vietnam	17	Stable
Thailand	16	Stable
Costa Rica	16	Rising slowly
Indonesia	10 (est.)	Stable
Paraguay	8	Declining
Ecuador	7	Rising slowly
Peru	5	Rising rapidly
Mexico	5	Stable
Guatemala	5	Rising slowly
El Salvador	5	Stable
Colombia	4	Stable
Nepal	4	Declining
Panama	3	Rising slowly
Honduras	2	Rising slowly

Source: Advisory Committee on Overseas Cooperative Development, *Farmer Cooperatives in Developing Countries* (Washington, D.C.: ACOCD, 1971), p. 14.

contrast, the very low percentages in the second group tell us that the cooperative is not being used as a way of creating the necessary conditions of access for the entire farm community.

Vertical Integration of Farmer Cooperatives

One of the misleading ideas in the development of farmer cooperatives is that a cooperative is mainly a local organization. The emphasis has been on organizing individual village societies. But the management of a financial system, the manufacture and distribution of fertilizer and other production inputs, most marketing and processing—these and other functions are much too big in scale for a local cooperative unit. These operations must be organized on a regional and/or national level, depending on the size and population of the country.

This means "vertical integration." In countries which have both modern agriculture and effective cooperatives, the real economic muscle of cooperatives is at the level of regional and national federations of local cooperatives. The local level is where farmers are organized and where farm decisions are made, but the business is mostly managed from above.

In the United States, for example, 1/3 of fertilizer sales, 2/3 of dairy marketing, 2/5 of grain and soybeans, about 1/3 of fruits and vegetables, and 1/4 of petroleum products used on farms are handled by cooperatives. The management of nearly all of this $17 billion a year business is handled through regional federations, although the retail distribution of supplies and collection of produce to be marketed is handled by the local cooperatives.

In Denmark virtually all agricultural marketing is handled by cooperatives. When it is said that, "for some purposes Denmark is one big farm,. . ."[12] the purposes are those of a federation, not local cooperatives. Efficient federations are the essential superstructure of a network of local cooperatives.

Table 5-4 shows how cooperatives are integrated vertically, through federations, in Taiwan and Uganda, and contrasts them with the common pattern of tiny, unfederated village societies in other developing countries.

In a number of countries the federations are more accurately described as "export marketing boards." They are a way of collecting produce from farmers for certain commodities grown primarily for the world market, such as coffee, cotton, and cocoa. They are not cooperative federations designed to help farmers benefit from genuine diversification and commercialization of agricultural production.

In the several countries in which federations market small quantities of foodgrains, farmers receive the same limited benefits as in the export systems. In India marketing federations are doing well in sugar, vegetable oils, and dairying. However, the village societies which produce these commodities are dominated by the larger and medium-sized farmers. A few countries have established federations in just the past several years. This is an encouraging, though somewhat belated, step.

In Asia and Africa, and to a lesser degree in Latin America, government agencies perform some of the functions of a federation, such as distributing fertilizer and marketing export crops.

A farmer who lacks access to the market as an individual is no better off by being a member of a village society if he still lacks access to the market. The all-important economies of scale, which are regional or national by the nature of their function, are denied to local cooperatives in many developing countries.

Table 5-4
Vertically Integrated and Ineffectively Integrated Farmer Cooperatives

The Economic Landscape	Taiwan	Uganda	Typical Pattern
National market	Provincial Federation of Farmers Associations, Ministry of Food, and Cooperative Bank	Cooperative Central Union, Ministry of Agriculture, and Cooperative Bank	Government agencies, such as Ministry of Agriculture, Registrar of Cooperatives, and a Cooperative Bank
Regional Market			Higher level field staff of central government agencies and often a marketing federation of some kind
District market (county)	22 county or city federations of Township Farmers' Associations	Federations of village societies	Lower level field staff of central government agencies
Local market (township or village clusters)	324 Township Farmers' Associations consisting of		Unorganized
	4854 small agricultural units (average of 15 per township)[a]	40 to 150 individual village cooperative societies	Unfederated individual village societies

Note: In larger countries there will be more than the three levels shown for Taiwan and Uganda. In Japan, for example, there is a Prefecturial (Regional) Federation.

[a]In the larger villages of Taiwan there may be more than SAU per village. Hence, the unit is not identical with the individual village societies shown in the other columns.

Yet, meaningful access for the small farmer makes cooperative federation essential. Without it his local unit will not have access to regional, national, and world markets. "The examples from developed countries clearly show that primary (local) cooperatives only become really effective when they form part of an integrated system of federations and unions."[13]

The Size of Local Cooperatives

Local cooperatives in most developing countries are weakened not only by a lack of strong federations but also by their own small size. Most are actually too small to be viable agricultural enterprises.

The size of the population and geographic base of the local cooperative are two of the significant differences between modernizing and dual society countries. In the former, the area of the local cooperative is either a cluster of villages (or township)—Japan, Taiwan, Israel, Egypt; or a county federation of village societies—Korea, Uganda, Comilla County. In other countries the area comprising the local cooperative is the individual village. The amount of economic activity in an area as large as a township or county is sufficient to support a viable business organization. The amount of economic activity in an area as small as a village is not sufficient for viability.

An example of a viable local cooperative unit is provided by Tan-tze, one of the 324 township cooperatives of Taiwan. In 1962 this cooperative had 2,100 members who cultivated 4,600 acres. They used 4,500 tons of fertilizer and produced 28,000 tons of crops. They deposited $1.4 million during the year, or $660 per member. Production loans totalled $360,000 or $172 per member. With this scale of activities the cooperative supported a staff of 33. It owned 9 warehouses and a rice mill and operated 3 supply stores.[14]

These quantities are mentioned not just to note that they are sufficient to achieve low unit costs in such things as transport, storage, and banking, but rather, to say that the volume of fertilizer, produce, and money made it possible to achieve a reasonable cost of operations. Such quantities are much larger than the sum of all transactions of a village cooperative.

The need to maintain a certain minimum size of operations has too often been ignored wherever local cooperatives have been organized in individual villages, which has been the common practice. Most villages in the developing countries have fewer than 1,000 people.

Countless thousands of villages have only several hundred people. A local cooperative with 50 or even 150 members is too small to survive. In India, for example, average membership in a village society is 150, only 7 percent of the membership of the Tan-tze cooperative in Taiwan. On the basis of average farm-size in India, the total area cultivated by the 150 members is only 825 acres. On the basis of the national average of fertilizer usage in 1970, the amount of fertilizer used is less than 100 tons. Its members do not purchase enough fertilizer, do not market enough food, do not handle enough money to approach the minimum volume of transactions needed to keep a modern cooperative farm business operating.[15]

Such a cooperative is too small to finance the needed facilities, too poor to hire a staff, and incapable of serving the members who need it most—the small farmers. Clearly, a business without adequate facilities, or a competent fulltime staff, is a business in name only.[b]

To some extent, North Americans and Europeans must share the blame for the countless village societies that litter the rural landscape. Thousands of them were organized in the 1950s with the help of the aid agencies during the heyday of the Traditional Community Development programs, discussed in chapter 2, by people who were not trained in either cooperative organization or agricultural business.

Unfortunately, these tiny village societies are far and away the most common form of local cooperatives in the developing countries today. Table 5-5 shows the average membership of local societies in 17 countries. The reader will note the great difference in the average size of the local units between the modernizing and dual society countries.

Countries and development assistance agencies that used separate and isolated village societies as a way of helping to organize the economic landscape (as discussed in chapter 3), to organize a modern agricultural system, and to give small farmers access to such a system failed to achieve any of these objectives. One consequence of the mistakes of the 1950s was a considerable reduction in the support of cooperative development by aid agencies, including the United States agency, a reduction that has persisted to the present time.

Land Tenure

The second aspect of access is land tenure. Land tenure systems are part of a rural social system and can be judged only in the context of such a system. Some of the statistics used to justify "land reform" in the developing countries are not so much a description of the existing system of land tenure as symptoms of a situation of highly structured inequality imbedded in rural society.

This means that an equitable distribution of land is not a *sine qua non* of agricultural development, provided that small freeholders and tenants as well as large farmers have access to the means of production, the financial system, the market, and knowledge. There are, however, two caveats to this generalization. In the first place, as we saw in chapter 4, there is now much evidence that a small farmer can be more efficient than a large farmer. An agricultural develop-

[b]The Royal Commission on the Cooperative Movement in Ceylon recently recommended that the number of village agricultural societies be reduced by about 90 percent by merging "from five to ten and often more existing rural societies" to form one viable unit. *Report of the Commission*, Government Publications Bureau, Colombo, 1970.

Table 5-5
Average Membership in Local Agricultural Cooperatives—Late 1960s

Country	Local Geographic Unit[a]	Average Membership
Modernizing		
Uganda	County Federation of Village Societies	16,665
Korea	County Federation of Village Societies	16,158
Comilla County	County Federation of Village Societies	11,673
Taiwan	Township	2,456
Japan	Township	998[b]
Dual Society		
Philippines	Farm Area Surrounding Market Towns	578
El Salvador	Village	525
Ceylon	Village	182
Peru	Village	169
Honduras	Village	164
Chile	Village	163
India	Village	150
Iran	Village	132
Panama	Village	98
Ecuador	Village	50
Thailand	Village	49
West Pakistan	Village	43

Source: Advisory Committee on Overseas Cooperative Development, *Farmer Cooperatives in Developing Countries* (Washington, D.C.: ACOCD, 1971), p. 16.

[a]For simplicity of presentation we have used North American names for the geographic areas involved. For some of the countries this familiar designation is an approximation rather than an accurate description that could be used in the country.

[b]Because of the relatively small size of many Japanese societies, the smaller ones are being merged into larger and more viable units.

ment strategy based on small farms appears to be the best way to raise both production and farm employment. Secondly, there is a possibility that technological advances in agriculture may endanger access for small farmers in an unequal land distribution system.

Given these caveats, let us now consider the significance of the social situation on land tenure systems. Tenancy, for example, is considered to be a major problem in a number of the poor countries. Tenancy, however, is not *ipso facto* a problem. In the 1930s the proportion of land farmed on a tenancy basis in the United States and in Japan was approximately 1/3 of cultivated land. In Britain it was even higher.

Similarly, so-called oral contracts between landowner and tenant do not necessarily mean the former is taking unfair advantage of the latter. Such contracts are still used in Illinois.

The existence of a large group of people who are called, in the language of development, "landless agricultural workers," is not *ipso facto* an argument for land reform (though it must be acknowledged that such farm workers are among the lowest income groups in all societies, including our own). A quarter of the United States farm labor force can be so described and the proportion in Britain is even higher.

Finally, before being aroused by the emotion which the twentieth century has attached to the words "landlord" and "moneylender," we should recall a most distinguished group of men, nearly all of them "landlords" and "money-lenders," who are more honorably known in history as our Founding Fathers.

This is not to dismiss lightly the extremes in land ownership that still exist in the Third World, primarily Latin America. In a world in which a certain measure of equitable distribution of income is endorsed almost universally, estates that are tens of thousands of acres (as still exist in some Latin countries) are indefensible.

The point is that the land tenure system is a major problem when large landlords are allowed to use their position to coerce and mistreat their smaller neighbors and deny them access to the agricultural system. Human beings should most assuredly not be so tied to the land that they can actually be bought and sold when the land is bought and sold—as in Bolivia prior to the land reform begun in 1952. Nor should people be deterred from improving their homes. "There was much new building of houses, which landowners had formerly forbidden"[16] (Iran). The worst feature of moneylending (which is of course an integral part of traditional land tenure systems) is not the high interest rates. Rather, in many parts of the world the system is a form of bondage, for the small farmer is not expected to pay off his debts. Perpetual indebtedness is a way of keeping in vassalage people who possess neither economic nor social power. *Le droit de seigneur* is another example of the social abuse of economic power.

These are the affronts to human dignity which must be ended if the marginal people are to benefit from development. They are aspects of a social system designed to institutionalize and perpetuate privilege and peonage. To be sure, some of the exploitation of the marginal people can be removed by changing them from tenants or sharecroppers to freeholders, but they will not become independent farmers unless the other conditions of access described previously are created. "Any integrated type of reform requires continuity in execution; expropriation must be followed by quick redistribution, and the functional organizations must be set up immediately, so that a new structure at once replaces the old."[17] The effectiveness of the "functional organizations" is a major reason why the land reforms of Japan, Taiwan, Korea, and Egypt were so successful.

This distinction between land ownership and the social situation is emphasized because there are many countries in which legislatures are controlled by landlords. Land redistribution is not politcally possible even though it is the preferred solution. But, it is also true that a great deal of social progress is possible without redistribution of the land. An enlightened aristocracy may not be willing to give up ownership of its estates, but it will create the conditions of access for tenants and small freeholders, as did Britain and Meiji Japan in the nineteenth century.

In other parts of the world as well as our own, equity is more difficult to achieve than a certain minimum level of opportunity. Creation of the latter is essential if the developing countries are to solve the human problems of development.

In land tenure the essential minimum level of opportunity is a "tenancy reform." By this is meant granting to the tenant certain rights to cultivate indefinitely a particular plot of land which the landlord is required to acknowledge in law, including a fixed annual rent. In particular, tenancy reform is a way of halting those abuses of a system of social inequity of which a few examples were given above. In Japan and Taiwan some decades ago tenancy reform gave the tenant the protection he needed to be willing to invest in modern technology and land improvement. Much more recently, tenancy reform in Ceylon and central Luzon in the Philippines appears to be inducing the same result among tenants.

Controversy over "land reform" is frequently a tactic used by vested interests to delay changes in the agricultural system. For example, the defenders of skewed land ownerships systems sometimes argue that under a small farm system the proportion of agricultural output that is marketed will decline on the grounds that small farmers consume most of what they grow whereas large farmers market most of what they grow. Following land redistribution, it is said, there would be less food for the urban population. Either city people would go hungry or else governments would need to use scarce foreign exchange, which should be spent for development projects, to import food.

The small farmers of Taiwan market about two-thirds of their output.[18] Considering the high levels of productivity achieved in Taiwan, this is perhaps not surprising. But the same is also true in Mexico—in both the large farm and *ejido* (land reform) portions of her agricultural dual economy. According to the Mexican agricultural census of 1960, the proportion of large farm production that was marketed was 67.7 percent. The same figure for the *ejido* portion was only a little less—65.2 percent.[19] Thus, the notion that land reform might cause a food shortage in the cities is another example of the mythology of inequity.

Thus, we conclude at this point that land redistribution, though obviously desirable, is not actually essential. But the conditions of access are essential. In most countries of Asia and Africa the largest single group of farmers are already small freeholders. If governments are willing, these farmers could be brought into the world of modern agriculture quickly.

Even in the Latin countries, one authority estimates that 60 percent of the farmers could be brought into the modern sector now in spite of the enormous inequities in land ownership and the huge numbers of landless agricultural workers.[20]

However, it could be that these conclusions need to be revised because of the following problem.

The Green Revolution is giving rise to a new problem of access to the land. It may be there is a Gresham's Law of farm size and system, namely: large-farm extensive and small-farm intensive farming cannot coexist in the same country,[c] the larger will drive out the smaller.[21] If there is such a law, then the large farm, large machinery policy of the Green Revolution countries may need to be reversed—a formidable political undertaking—if there is to be any chance at all of solving the employment problem.

Historically, it is a fact that the two types of farming do not coexist in the same country. In the successful small farm countries, governments have limited maximum farm size in accordance with the balance of the supply of land and farm labor. Thus, Japan and Taiwan not only redistributed the land but imposed a limit on farm size. In part this was considered to be a matter of equity, but in part these size limits represent a policy designed to maintain small farm, labor-intensive agriculture.

In Europe and North America there is great variation in farm size, and nowhere more than in our country. Even so, farming in Europe and North America is extensive in nature, based on labor-saving machinery. The type of small-scale, labor-intensive farming which is the essence of a Japanese-style agricultural revolution does not exist in our part of the world. Is the absence of extensive, capital-heavy farming in Japan, Taiwan, Egypt, and Korea, and the absence of small farm, labor-intensive farming in North America and Europe just a happenstance of history?

In India and other Green Revolution countries the larger farmers (25 acres or more; even as few as 25 acres constitutes at least a medium-sized farm in the crowded countries) are buying tractors and forcing their tenants off the land. Most of the ex-tenants become unemployed, except to the extent they can pick up casual jobs.

There appears to be a conflict of interest between the large farmer's desire to buy a tractor and the national need to create jobs. The large farmer may, indeed, increase his profits by using a tractor. In fact, however, it is extremely difficult to know whether this possible conflict is genuine today because the governments of a number of the Green Revolution countries are subsidizing the price of tractors, as explained in chapter 4 with regard to Pakistan. Nobody knows whether the large farmers would buy tractors if they were obliged to pay the true cost and if the domestic price level of wheat and rice at least approximated world prices.

This violation of the common sense of economics will not be found in the

[c]There is an important technical distinction which requires explanation here. We are not speaking of land ownership but farming units. A thousand acres can be cultivated with machinery as a single farm or cultivated as 200 five-acre farms on a tenancy basis. In this section we are concerned with the organization of farming units, not ownership.

early history of agricultural development in Japan and Taiwan. Rather, the opposite will be found. Farmers not only paid the costs of rural development—through taxation and other policies they helped finance the costs of industrial development as well. When the government intervened in the market to fix prices it was to keep the price of production inputs somewhat above the true market level in order to increase the transfer of investment funds from agriculture to industry.

One result of India's dual-economy agricultural policies, presumably accelerated by the Green Revolution, is an increase in the size of large farms. In the wheat area in northwestern India in the past fifteen years, the total amount of land owned by farmers with 20 to 25 acres increased by 4 percent. However, the area covered by large farms of 100 to 150 acres increased by no less than 40 percent.[22] Those who were forced to sell were the smaller farmers who could not compete with the larger farmers because they lacked access, especially credit on reasonable terms. They were (and are) being compelled to sell their little bits of land to pay off their debts.

The notion that large-farm extensive and small-farm intensive farming cannot coexist in the same modern agricultural system is implicit in the displacement of farm workers by large tractors which is now under way in the Green Revolution countries. As the large farmers increase their incomes they have the money to buy up the land of their smaller neighbors, and especially where small farmers are not yet a part of the modern agricultural system. Thus far, however, the question has not been studied in the manner expressed here. It requires study urgently. We need to know whether the present displacement of farm workers will cease when all the large farmers who want tractors have bought them; or, alternatively, whether the purchase of tractors represents the first step in a United States-style agricultural revolution in conditions which require a Japanese-style agricultural revolution.

Financial and Economic Discipline in Agriculture

Agricultural progress depends, in part, on organizing a system for mobilizing savings and channeling them into useful investments—land improvement, fertilizer, market and storage facilities, farm-to-market roads, processing plants, and others—a "system of capital formation," as economists call it.

To begin with the private sector: many countries have organized national agricultural development banks. However, the principal beneficiaries of these banks have been the larger farmers because governments have emphasized individual loans and commercial terms, i.e., sufficient collateral to secure the loans.

No country, however (including Europe and North America), has solved the farm credit problem through individual commercial loans. The risks are too high for regular, commercial banking because many farmers are unable to provide collateral to secure their loans, and because the cost of administering small loans is too high. Throughout the noncommunist world the institutional pattern of agricultural finance in the private sector is a combination of private banks and farmer cooperatives, with the government itself assuming a portion of the risk on production loans.

Thus far in history the only way in which the small farmers have been brought into a modern system of capital formation is by using the cooperative to promote thrift through deposits of savings and idle money, and by building member investment in share-capital.

Farmers require two types of capital for raising the output of their farms: seasonal financing of crop and livestock production, and permanent capital invested in land improvements, buildings, machinery, equipment, and animals.

Too often the problem of individual loans is considered to be just a matter of financing the costs of increasing production because credit funds are scarce. However, if the social power of the traditional moneylender is to be curbed—which it must be, as explained earlier—the villager must be able to borrow money for weddings, funerals, and other traditional or unexpected family expenses.

When villagers are hard pressed for cash, they borrow from whatever source they can. Thus, if the cooperative refuses or is unable to make personal loans, the villager may make a false application for a production credit or commodity loan, or failing that, turn to the local moneylender. The new personal loan system must meet both personal as well as production needs if the social problem of the villager is to be solved.

In developing countries the only agency from which most farmers can borrow adequate amounts for financing modern farm production at reasonable interest charges is the cooperative. However, the amount loaned a farmer is often inadequate to pay for the inputs to produce high yields. And sometimes, because of red tape, the money is paid too late for the farmer to use it.

Cooperatives also are usually the only agency from which small farmers can obtain intermediate and long-term loans because agricultural banks and government agencies generally require land as security. Farmers are everywhere reluctant to mortgage their land, and especially if they own very little. Further, well-run cooperatives have a much better loan collection record than agricultural banks and government lending offices. Collection rates in government lending programs are sometimes as low as only 70 percent, or even less. Apart from these points, neither farmers nor any other group in the community should be dependent indefinitely upon governments for credit.

Farmer cooperatives require funds for three purposes, individual loans for farmers, working capital, and fixed investment in facilities for such things as storage, marketing, transport, processing—the kinds of investment made by a cooperative as a group-business organization.

The needed capital can be obtained from four sources: government banks, commercial banks, individual members, and surpluses from the cooperative's activities as a group business.

Especially in the beginning, financial help from governments or development assistance agencies is needed because farmers will not be able to save much until their incomes begin to rise. In the long run, however, cooperatives should build up sufficient capital to finance their own operations or to be able to borrow on normal commercial terms.

That small farmers can save and build up capital has been demonstrated in Japan, Taiwan, and Korea and by successful regional or local cooperatives in other countries. In Taiwan, for example, the farmer cooperatives by 1968 were financing 4/5 of individual loans from their own resources.[23]

Capital formation in the above mentioned countries resulted from programs to induce deposits of savings and idle cash by members, long-term plans for building member investment in share-capital, and reinvestment of surpluses from business operations. Directors and officers learned how to determine the economic feasibility of proposed investments and how to plan the financing, including the investment required from members.

Without a definite plan for fostering capital formation, the growth of deposits and investment in share-capital in cooperatives will be far below that needed for financing the services required by farmer members. Developing countries that have not diligently promoted thrift in cooperatives have very small deposits, as shown in a survey of Asian countries. In the late 1960s, deposits in the local cooperatives of Japan averaged 84 percent of working capital; in Taiwan 76 percent, in Korea 50 percent. In other Asian countries deposits amounted to only 1/10 or less of working capital.

The total amount of deposits sheds more light on the relative amount of working capital available to farmers. In Korea average deposits per cooperative (county-based) were $670,000, in Taiwan (township-based) $380,000, and in Comilla County $195,000. In the village-based cooperatives of other Asian countries the amount of deposits per society averaged less than $400.[24]

Cooperatives almost everywhere require the purchase of one or several shares as a condition of membership. Few cooperatives, however, sell shares as a way of mobilizing capital or, the other way around, offering farmer-members a way of saving by investing in their cooperative.

The result of these inadequacies is that few cooperatives are accumulating needed capital. No less serious is that funds which are available for credit often are not coordinated with production inputs, or with access to the market, or with the dissemination of agricultural knowledge. "Consequently, credit does not contribute significantly to increases in land productivity and farm incomes."[25]

This contravention of the basic tenets of financial discipline is common in developing countries. Yet, financial discipline must be followed if small farmers are to pay the cost of their own improvement.

Hence, we now turn to the question of creating financial discipline among extremely poor farmers.

The basic financial principle of cooperative finance has always been, in sequence, savings, credit worthiness, loans. In agriculture, establishing credit worthiness is a combination of two things: first, a character reference from one's neighbors, that is, the members of the credit and finance committee of the local cooperative; and second, a simple version of a farm plan approved by someone of technical competence, that is, the local extension agent or the crop production committee of the local cooperative.

In the beginning the emphasis should be on the discipline of a financial system, for savings cannot be high where farm incomes are low and static. Consider the example of Comilla County, "During April, 1960, savings of the first seven (village) agriculture societies ranged from $2.85 to $15.50. The per-member monthly savings ranged from 12 cents to 63 cents."[26] From the outset, members were required to make a weekly savings deposit as a condition of membership, no matter how small. The members of the vegetable growers' society were required to deposit 1/16 of the amount of each sale. The maximum loan a farmer could receive was determined, in part, by his savings. This sometimes led to the paradox of a farmer borrowing money to increase his savings account so that he could obtain a larger loan to buy all the fertilizer that he needed. Private bankers also insist on requirements of this type. No banker will lend money to a person who proposes to invest nothing at all in his project. Yet, agricultural loans in the Third World are frequently made on this basis.

These and similar requirements were intended to force farmers in Comilla County to save as a condition of outside help. In the beginning, outside help was 4/5 of the investment in particular projects. The total amount of investment per acre was low. But priming the pump is one of the functions of governments. Now, ten years later, the County federation of village societies owns two cold storage plants, a creamery, a rice mill, some transport equipment, and warehouses. Total individual savings now exceed $140,000 per year. Gross assets of the County federation, which consists of 301 village agricultural societies and 77 nonagricultural societies, are now $5 million.[27]

Part of the significance of Comilla County is the extreme poverty in this region. It is located in one of the most crowded areas of the world. The population density of the county is almost 2,000 per square mile. The average farm is only 1.7 acre. When the cooperative was started per capita income was estimated at $40 to $50 per year. Nevertheless, the project was based on the harsh financial discipline of compulsory savings.

How the disciplined, modernizing cooperative has affected the villagers of Comilla is illustrated by the following story:

With the introduction of the cooperative and improved methods of cultivation, some people in the village have become very active. Before the introduction of the cooperative, he himself was an idle and lazy person. He spent most of his time gossiping. Now his whole way of life has changed. He cultivates his land using improved methods, has learned new skills and habits, and knows how to save money, use fertilizers, insecticides, weeders, etc.[28]

It is also worth noting, or rather, emphasizing, that "with the increased demand for labor the tendency of labor to move out of the village has been reduced, as is evidenced by the fact that no family has left during the last two years."[29]

Uganda is another example of the rapidity with which savings and investment can be increased. In the Ankole District[d] total funds available for production credit increased 4 times between 1965 and 1969 and the proportion of borrowed capital declined from 78 to 29 percent. The cooperative's own funds increased 12 times, from $12,000 to $140,000. There was a fourfold increase in personal savings.

In addition, over the five-year period members of the 77 village societies which make up the District Union voted to forego dividend payments of $78,000 in order to build capital.[30]

Beginning small illustrates an important characteristic of much of agricultural investment. It can be made in very small increments. A farmer can use some fertilizer one year and a little more the next. A farmer cooperative can continue to use traditional methods of storage until it can finance an improved warehouse. Hence, it is possible to initiate agricultural development with little capital and to advance as additional sums can be saved or borrowed.

One of the many attitudinal problems in the developing countries is that the tradition-oriented rich who control governments do not believe that the poor can save.

History offers evidence that the rich are wrong. In the countries mentioned in this chapter small farmers have demonstrated their ability to save money to increase production, which in turn leads to higher savings and consumption. They have invested in irrigation systems, fertilizer and other production inputs. They have also built permanent homes to replace their traditional flimsy shelters. They have been able to afford a variety of household furnishings and other consumer goods (increased demand for local factories), better education, and health and other improvements.

All of these things are possible if productivity and, hence, farm incomes, are rising continuously. Rising productivity and market development are the key to rural savings and increased consumption. No matter how poor a person may seem to be in the eyes of the rich, if his income is rising he can be persuaded to save and invest a portion of the increase.

But these savings can be mobilized and put to productive use only if there is a local financial institution. "The major problem of capital accumulation in underdeveloped economies is not so much a shortage of savings but a lack of institutions to channel the existing or latent surplus into productive investment."[31]

---

[d]A district in Uganda is the equivalent of a rather large, mid-West county in the United States. There are 17 districts in the country.

One of the quickest ways to distinguish between modernizing and dual society governments is to examine the financial system for small farmers. Modernizing governments believe small farmers can pay the cost of their own improvement and therefore organize a system of capital formation. Dual society governments lack confidence that poor families can become independent farm producers. By failing to organize a system of capital formation they help to make their prediction come true.

Taiwan, for example, has already built up enough capital so that the local cooperatives are no longer primarily dependent on government for credit funds for production loans. Korea is approaching this same situation. Ceylon, Uganda, and Comilla County are building up a system that can yield the same result if the progress of recent years is continued.

At the present time the amount of production credit available to farmers in most developing countries depends primarily on how much money the government is able to allocate. The excessive dependency of cooperatives on the public treasury will continue until and unless governments are willing to apply the time-tested tenets of financial discipline in cooperatives—savings, credit-worthiness, loans.

The lack of discipline in the private sector financial system is, alas, paralleled by a similar lack in the public sector. One result is that governments are unable to raise the funds needed for land improvement, farm-to-market roads, schools, pump-priming the agricultural credit system, and other purposes where government financial help is needed.

A second result of this lack of discipline is almost a separate subject. It is included here because of the crucial role of governments in introducing economic discipline into an agricultural system.

Economic pressure can and should be applied to induce individual farmers to improve their efficiency. In the crowded countries there ought to be no place for the kind of inefficient farming which would, in a normal market, result in bankruptcy. This kind of inefficiency persists because the subsistence farmer still lives outside of the market economy, as explained in the first chapter.

Japan and Taiwan are examples of how governments can use tax and price policy both to raise investment funds and to apply pressure to farmers to increase productivity. "The importance of agriculture's contribution to the financing of industrial development in Japan is abundantly clear. Agriculture's share of tax revenue was on the order of 85 percent during the years 1888-92 and still accounted for some 40 percent in 1918-22. . . . The government outlays to extend and improve the rail network and for other types of infrastructure to establish 'model' factories, and to subsidize the fledgling merchant marine and the shipbuilding industry were particularly significant."[32] At that time taxes were 15 to 20 percent of a farmer's income. The land tax was especially high.

Much more recently Taiwan has imposed economic discipline in public sector finance. The principal tax paid by farmers is the land tax, which is based on a combination of the quality of the soil (there are 26 grades of rice land) and actual production. The rate is progressive, varying from 3.5 to 9.6 percent of the value of production. Rising productivity means higher taxes. The tax varies from as little as 25¢ per acre on poor soil, poorly farmed, to $10 and $20 an acre on well-farmed, fertile land.[33]

On price policy, the Taiwan government has deliberately maintained high prices for production inputs. Until the late 1960s fertilizer was as expensive in Taiwan as anywhere in the world and several times more costly than in the advanced countries.

Three highly desirable results of this financial and economic discipline in Taiwan are:

1. Farmers have been under pressure to use modern inputs and techniques in order to increase their income to pay their taxes. Those farmers who became freeholders under the land reform program also had to meet the annual installment on their land purchase. The combination of the two was as high as 37.5 percent of the farmer's income. Thus, in spite of the exceptionally high price of fertilizer, the use of fertilizer has been higher in the past two decades than in any other developing country.
2. The Taiwan government has been able to raise sufficient revenue to finance the irrigation systems, rural road networks, and other activities which are usual functions of government around the world.
3. There long has been a net transfer of resources out of agriculture to help finance industrialization. During the 1960s this averaged about $20 per year per farm worker.[34]

Thus, in public finance as well as private finance, Taiwan has demonstrated the discipline needed to increase savings in order to increase investment which, in turn, increases incomes.

In contrast to Taiwan, "the real burden of agricultural land taxes has been greatly reduced in many of the underdeveloped countries as a result of failure to adjust tax rates in accordance with the rise in price levels since World War II."[35] For example, prior to the war the land tax was more than one-fifth of the revenue of undivided India. Since the tax rates per acre are essentially unchanged, today the land tax is less than 3 percent, although the requirements for investment are much higher than in the late 1930s when the world was not yet conscious of "development." The land tax averaged only 35¢ an acre in the mid-1960s, and farmers paid only 1.5 percent of their income in taxes.[36]

Of the generally unsatisfactory level of agricultural taxation, one eminent economist has written: "The remedy for this is decentralization of services to local authorities. Farmers resent paying taxes for which they may get no return. However, if the services are provided by local authorities under their control, to whom the taxes are paid, the farmers can see what they are getting for their money, and are more willing to give voluntary labor as well as pay more taxes to meet their own needs. Decentralization thus raises taxable capacity. The thesis popularized by western sociologists and political scientists that economic development requires highly centralized government is a dangerous myth."[37]

The result of the kind of policies described above is that farmers are under no pressure to improve their efficiency, and governments are unable to finance essential investments. Having said this, however, there is one caveat: economic pressure should not be applied to individual farmers unless the conditions of access have already been created. Otherwise, farmers, and especially the smaller ones, will be driven off the land in search of jobs that do not exist.

The Pace of Farmer Development

The pace of development should be set primarily by the farmers themselves. Farming is a precarious business in any country. It is especially precarious when farms are so small that a mistake on a single acre can mean hunger or economic hardship. Farmers will be wary of adopting modern technology unless they are confident they know how to use it on their own land in their own way. Farmers will also be wary if they are uncertain whether they can sell their increased production in order to recoup the costs of using modern technology. By now subsistence farmers have had enough contact with the modern world to know that higher production is possible. They also know that fertilizer and other modern inputs increase the costs of production. If they have purchased fertilizer on credit and then cannot sell their greater output, they may not be able to repay their debts. This could mean a loss of a portion of their land. Pushing the debtor off the land is a centuries-old way through which landlords have increased the size of their holdings at the expense of the small farmer.

Lack of market development may well be a greater deterrent to higher productivity than the uncertainty involved in using new and different methods of production, for the farmer can always test the latter on a tiny bit of his land in order to learn how to use them. Indeed, many Asian farmers have asked in the course of conversations about increasing agricultural production, "Where would I sell it?"

A strategy of agricultural development based on a succession of small improvements which the small farmer can adjust to, one by one, and each requiring only a modest increase in investment, may turn out to be a faster way of achieving high levels of productivity than an occasional abrupt change requiring a heavy increase in investment, such as the miracle seeds.

To say these things is not to say that governments should not suggest or even apply pressure to accelerate. The problem for governments is to listen, to learn how farmers think. This is partly a matter of governments having confidence in farmers, of believing that villagers know more about farming conditions in their own community than the outsider—know more, in other words, than the government knows. It is partly a matter of creating the relatively autonomous local institutions in which farmers are allowed to solve their personal and community problems.

Rather than elaborate on these points we shall again use a comparison of country performance to illustrate the advantage of trusting and investing in small farmers. First, "one of the principal lessons to be derived from the Japanese [and also, Taiwan, Egypt, Korea] is the importance of progressively modifying farming systems rather than attempting the wholesale substitution of 'modern' for 'traditional' agriculture."[38] But there is a much more recent example.

In the hubbub of the Green Revolution, the performance of one small Asian country, Ceylon, has been hardly noticed. Ceylon has not yet adopted wholeheartedly the small farm-market town, agro-industry policy being discussed in this book; and there is a measure of the "dual economy" in that her export crops (tea, rubber, and coconut) are primarily plantation agriculture. However, 94 percent of the rice farms are 5 acres or less. The government has adopted a rice production policy based on small farm, labor-intensive agriculture using "improved seeds" but not the "miracle seeds."

Many countries have "improved seeds" in the sense that some indigenous seeds are known to be more productive than the seeds which traditionally the farmer saved from this year's harvest for next year's planting. Plant breeders in Ceylon have been trying to improve these local varieties which are known to be resistant to local diseases and suitable to the local environment. These are varieties which the local farmers are accustomed to growing. The question long has been not whether such improved seeds existed—in some countries they have been available for decades. The question is whether the rural society of a country possesses the capacity to apply scientific knowledge that is available and known to be suited to its physical environment (climate, soil, water, and so forth). The rural societies of Taiwan and Egypt, not to mention Denmark, the United States, and other developed countries, possess this capacity. The dual rural societies of the Green Revolution countries, such as Mexico, India, and the Philippines have most conspicuously not demonstrated this capacity to adopt and adapt to continuous small improvements. Foodgrain productivity in these countries was virtually static throughout the whole of this century until the so-called "miracle seeds" were introduced to the large commercial farmers.

The rural society of Ceylon has begun to demonstrate this same capacity for gradual change. The organization of the small farmers and the introduction of the necessary financial discipline is under way, through the cooperative technique of organizing both farmers and systems. Rice yields now exceed 2000 pounds per acre. This is more than a third higher than in India and the Philippines. It is too soon to know whether this gradual and continuous rise in rice productivity will turn out to be the first step in the development of a modern, commercial agriculture in Ceylon. However, it is worth saying that improved rice farming was the beginning of agricultural progress in Japan, Taiwan, and Korea.

The Food and Agriculture Organization (FAO) of the United Nations describes Ceylon's policy as follows:

The essence of the strategy followed in Ceylon has been the adoption of a local improved variety of rice which, because it demands an intermediate level of technology requiring less cost, less risk and less labor discipline than the new high-yielding varieties, is assimilable by a wide base of small holdings. This strategy, however, requires relatively more in the line of an integrated set of incentives, institutions and services. In Ceylon as much as 72 percent of the paddy land in the main crop season 1969 was planted to the local improved varieties, H4 and H8, and yields have risen rapidly since 1965. Those proposing this strategy suggest that, where the necessary institutional framework is provided, it gives rise to a broader, quicker and more sustained increase in productivity, as has been demonstrated earlier by Japan and China [Taiwan]. They also point out that the initial adoption of the intermediate level of technology can pave the way for a more sophisticated technology at a later stage. The rationale of this approach is that, as a national strategy to obtain the highest increase in production, the aim need not necessarily be the attainment of the highest possible yields on individual holdings or in parts of the country, but the achievement of the highest possible average yield on a countrywide basis. The width of the production base also has implications. In the light of emerging economic and social conflicts in the wake of the green revolution in some countries such a strategy might therefore have social and political advantages in the long run.[39]

Figure 5-1 compares yields per acre in Ceylon with the Philippines and India. The reader will note that yields in the former are higher and rising more rapidly than in the latter. For purposes of comparison Taiwan is also shown on the graph. We might also note that yields in Japan have reached 5000 pounds per acre, in the United States not quite 4500 pounds.

Figure 5-2 on fertilizer usage also supports our contention that the national average is higher when all farmers advance in modest measure than when a few farmers advance rapidly. Fertilizer usage in Ceylon is several times higher than in any of the dual-economy countries, including Mexico, where land reform and agricultural development programs can be traced back for almost half a century. The figure also shows the enormous consumption of fertilizer in small-farm, labor-intensive agriculture in comparison to a large-farm country, such as the United States.

Agricultural development in the poor countries offers an unusual challenge. To the extent that country experience is a guide to policy today, we Americans who hope to help in this process must unlearn much of our own experience with large farm, highly mechanized agriculture and instead learn how to organize small farm, labor-intensive agriculture.

"The implications of the Japanese experience would appear to be so obviously valid that it would seem to be a foregone conclusion that today's developing

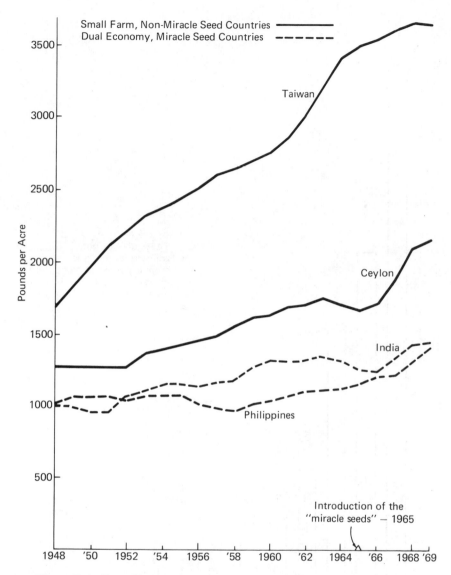

Figure 5-1. Rice Yields per Acre, 1948–1969. (The figures on which this graph is based are "three year moving averages" for each year, that is, each figure is the average of the year stated, the preceding year and the following year. This is a common practice in calculating agricultural productivity statistics since it evens out somewhat the seasonal fluctuations which are characteristic of agriculture) Source; FAO, *Production Yearbook*, 1948–1969, and *World Crop Statistics* (Rome, FAO, 1966).

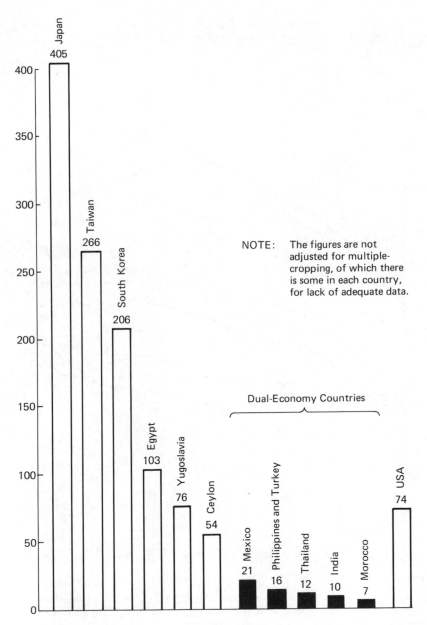

Figure 5-2. Fertilizer Consumption, 1969-1970. (Pounds Fertilizer Nutrient per Acre). Source: FAO, *Production Yearbook*, 1970.

countries would be pursuing comparable strategies of agricultural development. That this is not the case points to the need for better understanding of the reasons for the general tendency for developing countries [and the development assistance agencies] to underinvest in the institution-building that is a necessary condition for exploiting the potential that exists for expanding agricultural output at a low cost."[40]

6 Industrializing the National Economy

The key issues in industrial policy are similar to those in agriculture: how to involve the mass of small producers, increase production, and create jobs. An excess of subsidized machinery in a few factories—creating too few jobs—is the common pattern of industrial investment in the developing countries. But three other issues come to the fore in industrial policy that are not present in agriculture:

1. *The location of industry.* Must new factories be located in the few big cities? Or can they be efficiently spread throughout the national economy so as to prevent the stifling conglomeration of Calcutta, Lagos, or Sao Paulo, and to provide better service to the rural areas where the bulk of the people in the Third World live?
2. *The type of goods produced.* Should investment be concentrated on luxury products for the small wealthy elite or on basic necessities (textiles, shoes, utensils, furniture and so on) that are purchased by the majority?
3. *The relationship between agriculture and industry.* How can industrial growth best complement the type of rural regeneration discussed in the previous chapter?

In large measure these issues overlap. Our definition of broad-based development comprehends them all. More efficient use of resources, faster economic growth, and more jobs all require more use of labor and less of capital. This can be achieved in part by policies encouraging the adaptation of technology to fit labor abundant, capital scarce economies, and in part by emphasizing investment in goods bought by the poor, which are generally more labor-intensive in production. At the same time, the poor must be given the means to buy more goods: this means more and better jobs, especially in agriculture.

There is a certain group of factories frequently called "agro-industries" which are essential for agricultural growth. Agriculture cannot advance very far unless there are factories which produce the modern production inputs (fertilizer, pesticides, improved seeds, tools and machines, feedgrains) and also factories which process the much higher production which the production inputs make possible. However, both the developing countries and the aid agencies have tended to assume that 'rural development' is synonymous with increased agricultural production. Increasing output on the farm is only half the problem. Rural economic development is actually a combination of farm and certain types of industrial enterprises. Generally speaking, the developing countries have yet to link agricultural and industrial development so that an increase in demand in the one sector will induce increased supply in the other. In addition, most of the countries have ignored the rural consumer goods market, which, as we shall see, differs from the big city consumer goods market.

Broadly speaking, "agro-industries," consumer goods factories, and many other business establishments which by nature of their size and economic function logically fit into regional and local market areas, tend to be small, capital-saving and labor-intensive. A million dollars invested in small, or often more accurately, "tiny" business, will create several times as many jobs as a million dollars invested in a large, capital-intensive, city-oriented factory. Creating the conditions of access for small entrepreneurs in small cities and market towns will bring into the national economy countless thousands of new investors who, like small farmers, are not yet much involved in development. By thus creating jobs where people live now, migration to metropolis can be slowed down to manageable proportions.

Small industries also economize on scarce managerial talent because management is simple and direct. At the same time, they provide the opportunity for large numbers of small investors to acquire what the countries need most of all—experience and skill in management. In addition, the wages paid to the workers in small industries help to build up the buying power needed for consumer markets.

If we accept the premise that development should consist of a continuous succession of small advances, millions of individual actions by millions of individual people, then small, much more than large industry, suits the psychology of people in transition from traditional to modernized methods of production. Management is personal. The working situation is more flexible and can be adjusted more easily to seasonal demands. Personal relationships are more informal. Direct contact can be maintained with customers. In short, "the transition from an individualistic peasant life, where the rhythm of activity is ruled by the seasons, is made easier."[1]

Conspicuous Industrialization

But these are not the ideas on which industrial growth in the poor countries has been constructed. Generally speaking, their factories tend to be duplicates of North American or European factories with little adaptation to the conditions of the country, to its raw materials, labor skills, repair facilities, supply of capital, particularly foreign exchange, and so forth. Some such factories are part of the long-term process of industrialization, but they are only a part of a country's system of industrial production. Like the main-line railway and the high voltage transmission line, they belong to the national level of the national economy. In addition, this type of industrialization introduces the social divisions of a dual society into the labor force. "In countries where industrialization is in progress, the employees of modern large-scale factories are liable to become an aristocracy of labor. Between them and the majority of people who are left behind in the march of progress, there lie wide differences in wages and living standards. Big factories are so limited in number that they can absorb only a small fraction of the labor force."[2]

Sometimes these "modern" factories do not even achieve their intended economic purpose of augmenting national income, as the following illustrates:

One country imported two plastic injection-moulding machines costing $100,000 with moulds. Working three shifts and with a total labour force of forty workers they produced 1.5 million pairs of plastic sandals and shoes a year. At $2 a pair these were better value (longer life) than cheap leather footwear at the same price. Thus, 5,000 artisan shoemakers lost their livelihood; this, in turn, reduced the markets for the suppliers and makers of leather, hand tools, cotton thread, tacks, glues, wax and polish, eyelets, fabric linings, laces, wooden lasts and carton boxes, none of which was required for plastic footwear. As all the machinery and the material for the plastic footwear had to be imported, while the leather footwear was based largely on indigenous materials and industries, the net result was a decline in both employment and real income within the country.[3]

What is weakest, then, in industry, as in agriculture, is development at the regional and especially the local levels of the national economy. In part this is the result of government policies which favor big-city type factories. In part, small entrepreneurs, like small farmers, still lack access to the national production system. Yet there are many factories, and also many types of commercial activities and personal service industries, whose natural location is the regional and local urban centers discussed earlier.

Given the known historical importance of small business and geographically dispersed economic activities in the Western countries and notably in Japan, why have the developing countries over-emphasized capital-intensive, city-oriented factories?

To some extent, the explanation can be found in the well-known urban bias and "Western" orientation of policy makers and planners. This is combined frequently with a lack of personal knowledge of village and rural life in their own countries—characteristics which are reinforced by the essentially urban and machine-oriented North American and European advisors. "The managers, engineers, technicians, and even the planners trained abroad are often so convinced of the superiority of mechanized techniques, or so advised by the foreign consulting firms of engineers about the superiority of such techniques, that they readily discard the more labor-intensive techniques."[4] Further, not nearly enough is known or being learned about the type of technology which is needed in the developing countries. Ninety-nine percent of world expenditure on technological development takes place in the advanced countries, only 1 percent in the developing countries.[5] How this 99 percent is used depends on the situation of the advanced countries—the stage of development they have reached already, the relative prices of machines and labor, the problems the public considers important, the areas where scientists believe breakthroughs in the application of new knowledge are imminent. Not nearly enough is being done to adapt existing or new knowledge to the particular circumstances of the developing countries, which are, it hardly needs to be said, very different from the circumstances of the rich countries.

Because of too much mechanization of industrial production, employment in manufacturing in most developing countries is rising slowly. In Asia, between 1955 and 1967, manufacturing output, starting from a very small base, increased by four times, but employment by only 3/4.[6] In Latin America, from 1958 to 1967, factory output increased by 2/3, employment by only 1/4.[7] The number of jobs created per dollar of new investment is slowly declining because of more sophisticated technology and because many of the countries are shifting from light to heavy engineering, which requires relatively more money and creates fewer jobs than most other types of industrial investment.

The adverse effect of the concentration of investment in too few factories on job creation in Latin America is shown in table 6-1. The table is based on Raul Prebisch's excellent analysis of "the distortion in the structure of labor force" in his recent report on development in Latin America. Prebisch drew an historical parallel between certain Western countries and Latin America today.[8] Table 6-1 shows that the proportion of workers productively employed in factories is very much lower in Latin America today than at a roughly comparable stage of development in the West, that is, when the proportion of the total labor force working in agriculture was 42 percent, this being the proportion in Latin America at the time of Prebisch's study. But even worse, the proportion of workers employed in industry in Latin American is declining when it should be rising!

Table 6-1
Industrial Employment When Agricultural Employment was 42% of the Total Labor Force

	Year of 42% Agricultural Employment	Industrial Employment as % of Total Labor Force in 42% Year	Trend in Industrial Employment Around Time of 42% Year
United States	1890	28	Rising
Sweden	1924	35	Rising
France	1921	33	Rising
Italy	1950	30	Rising
Latin America	1969	19	Falling

Source: Derived from a table in Raul Prebisch, *Change and Development* (Washington, D.C.: Inter-American Development Bank, 1970), p. 30.

A large portion of those who cannot find a job in factories seek employment in the "services"—public utilities, transport, commerce and finance, government, and a great variety of personal services. The share of the labor force engaged in these occupations should increase in the course of development, but in Latin America the share has increased much too rapidly. The street vendors, the shoe shine boys, the parking attendants whom one "hires" so that his car will not be stripped of its removable parts—these "are for the most part the marginal population, in the strict sense of the term, namely people who have broken their links with rural life but have not yet managed to become an integral part of the ordinary life of the cities. They seek out an impoverished existence—in ever-increasing numbers, it seems—in the shanty towns which are a characteristic feature of the large urban agglomerations in Latin America."[9] How to employ this mass of marginal people is the central theme of Prebisch's report.

The fondness of too many governments for "prestige" factories is misplaced. They might better follow the humbler policy of Japan in the first decades of her modernization. "If Japan's experience teaches any single lesson regarding the process of economic development in Asia, it is the cumulative importance of myriads of simple improvements in technology which do not depart radically from tradition or require large units of new investment."[10]

It is this general policy that has been pursued by the modernizing countries. The countries which have had the fastest increase in manufacturing output are precisely those that have adopted prices for capital and labor that reflect their relative supply and that have created the conditions of access for entrepreneurs in regional and local urban centers as well as metropolis. They have also adopted the policies needed to induce investment in the "agro-industries" and the rural consumer market. In Taiwan, manufacturing output increased by 16 percent a year during the 1960s, almost triple the Third World average of just over 6 percent a year. Korea and Egypt (up until the Six Days War) did approximately as well. In each of these countries, manufacturing employment has risen by around 10 percent a year.

India and Brazil, however, have been investing in steel mills and other heavy engineering factories—the typical policy of a dual economy. These kinds of factories require relatively large amounts of capital and create rather few jobs. They are the factories of metropolis, not small cities and market towns. They contribute little to the creation of a mass market, or to the integration of agricultural and industrial development. In India manufacturing output during the 1960s rose by 5 percent every year, in Brazil (1960-67) a little less (in the last several years, output has been rising more rapidly in Brazil primarily because of an influx of foreign capital for large-scale plants: the employment impact of this is still unclear though likely to be limited). Unemployment and underemployment are major problems in both countries.

The way in which excessive mechanization of industry worsens the employment problem can be shown by comparing the number of jobs created by industrial investment in Japan and the Philippines. In both countries in 1965 the amount of capital invested per factory worker was about the same—$2,600.[11] If each country has $26 million to invest in new factories, then 10,000 new jobs would be created. However, in Japan, the amount of money available for factory investment is many times higher than in the Philippines.

First of all, per capita income in Japan is 6 times higher than in the Philippines. This means that if the proportion of income being invested in new factory jobs is the same in each country, Japan can create 6 new jobs while the Philippines is creating just one. However, the proportion of income being invested is not the same in each country. It is 60 percent higher in Japan. Thus, with the combination of much higher incomes and a higher rate of investment (as economists call it) Japan can create ten times as many factory jobs as the Philippines for a labor force that is increasing 1/3 as fast!

An Alternative Industrial Strategy

In discussing agriculture, we saw that relatively small amounts of capital spread thinly across the whole farming population, rather than the concentration of expensive machines on a few farms, is one essential policy of rapid agricultural progress (not to mention the enormous social advantages of putting people to work). The same point applies to industry as well, and the advantages are similar. Many more people are encouraged to invest. More jobs are provided, creating a mass market. And the technology used is adapted to local conditions.

We all know that machines are the way of increasing production, but this does not mean that machines need to be concentrated in a single place, such as a city-oriented factory. It means that more machines need to be used than are being used now—at all levels of the economy, regional and local as well as national, and by the mass of small producers as well as the handful of large ones.

There are, in fact, many examples of this already occurring: what is needed is a conscious policy of government support. Thus, in small cities of Pakistan today, blacksmiths are setting up 2 to 5 man shops to manufacture irrigation pumps at an equipment cost[a] of $800 to $2000.[12] This investment represents a considerable increase in the use of machines and in the productivity of labor over the traditional hand methods of metal working. However, these shops are capital-saving and labor-intensive in comparison to big city factories. They are one example, from industry, of the point emphasized in our discussion of agriculture, of how certain types of inexpensive machines can increase the amount of work done by hand and therefore create large numbers of jobs at a relatively low cost. They are also an example of how market towns and small cities can be industrialized.

The first step in the industrialization of the hinterland is to adjust the price

---

[a]At official exchange rates: the true cost is probably no more than half these amounts.

structure to reflect the scarcity of capital, especially foreign exchange, and the abundance of labor. This must, of course, be done country by country since the relative supply of capital and labor is everywhere different, as is also the political situation in which these economic decisions will be made. Since the analysis of the issues is both complex and technical, we shall not pursue the matter beyond the hopefully simplified explanation of the nature of the problem given in chapter 4.

Apart from the reasonable price structure which is needed if investing in small-scale industries is to be profitable, there are other aspects of the access problem which must be solved, as the following suggests.

In a town in northern India, small "manufacturers are versatile and resourceful with the few resources at their command. If they cannot buy a machine, they will build it themselves. If they cannot reproduce a technique, they will improvise one of their own. The small industrialists of Chopur have every earmark of the successful industrial entrepreneur, *except success*." The principal problem of these businessmen, at the time this study was done in 1956, was lack of working capital—the businessman's equivalent of a farmer's production credit. Yet, in the "hundreds of small machine shops scattered throughout North Indian towns, . . . there lies an enormous potential waiting to be tapped."[13] Thirteen years later this type of access problem still persisted in India.[14]

In Pakistan, the smallest of the pump manufacturers referred to above, pay twice as much for some of their raw materials as the larger firms.[15] The latter are big enough to qualify for an import license that enables them to buy imported pig iron at special prices. Because of other advantages, and in particular their ability to meet customers' exact requirements with quick delivery, the smaller manufacturers are able to compete anyway, but they should certainly not be penalized on raw materials prices because they are small.

If we may digress for a moment, government officials and economic planners in Pakistan seem to have been unaware of the pump manufacturing industry until it had already grown up, by which time there were more than 500 companies employing 6500 workers with an annual output in excess of $15 million (at the official exchange rate). Such lack of knowledge of local initiative is not uncommon in dual society countries where governments have failed to create a two-way communications system and where officials try to "plan" economic development without involving people.[16]

Many small firms have shown great ingenuity in overcoming problems of design, market development, and training, through tailoring their products to their customers' needs, through on-the-job apprenticeship schemes, and so on. But if these businesses are to flourish in large numbers, then the government must play a role in helping to provide these essential services, in much the same way as in agriculture. The effect of creating favorable economic policies in conjunction with some of the needed services can be seen in the rapid growth of small industry in Taiwan. In 1961, the island contained 52,152 industrial enterprises, of which 88 percent had been established within the previous ten years. All but 2 percent employed fewer than 50 workers.[17] It is primarily through these small firms that agricultural and industrial development have been linked and the market towns industrialized in Taiwan.

Avoiding Metropolitan Concentration

These are the kinds of problems that now prevent small traditional entrepreneurs from becoming modern producers. Given a willingness to solve them, getting industry out of metropolis is a combination of small business, agro-industries, and developing the village and small town consumer market. These three subjects overlap considerably, but they are not identical. Not all agro-industries are small, the fertilizer factory being one obvious exception. Not all small businesses are located in small cities and market towns, and not all are directly related to agriculture. In the Philippines, for example, 20 percent of the very small factories are located in Manila. The point is that the other 80 percent are scattered about the country in urban centers of various size. It is through the type of industries which make up the 80 percent that agricultural and industrial development can be integrated and the rural consumer market expanded. Generally speaking, these are the type of industries that require less capital and more labor than city-oriented capital-intensive factories. In addition, nearly all of the raw materials are local, not imported.

Agro-industries are usually defined as those industries which manufacture agricultural inputs—fertilizer, pesticides, improved seeds, tools, and machinery—and factories which use food, fibre, animal and wood products as raw materials. Without these factories agricultural progress will be sharply limited. Either the farmer will not be able to purchase the inputs needed for higher production or else he will have no market for the sale of his higher production.

However, we prefer a broader definition of agro-industries. The problem is not just a matter of using certain types of factories to integrate agricultural and industrial development, though that is the starting point. The problem is the creation of a variety of industries and services that people will want in a prospering rural community. Hence, we would add to the two categories of factories directly related to agricultural production four other groups: some consumer goods that can be manufactured efficiently in local shops, such as pens, pencils, domestic utensils, small tools and machines, some clothing, bicycles, soap, nails, sandals, matches; building materials, such as finished lumber, door and window frames, bricks and cement blocks, household furniture and furnishings; a great variety of personal services such as repair, electricians, tailors, laundries; and finally, certain luxury goods such as cosmetics, jewelry, mirrors, confections, and toys. These and many others are products and services which rural people will need and want as their incomes rise.

The modernizing countries have adopted the policies needed to stimulate this great array of industrial and commercial activity in local and regional areas. Government industrial investment banks are decentralized so that local entrepreneurs can obtain credit for both investment and working capital and also licenses, where these are necessary. With or without government help, private banks have sprung up as the level of economic activity has risen. In Taiwan, for example, there are now two financial institutions per township—a private bank and the farmer cooperative. In most countries there are still only one or two private banks per province. Technical assistance is provided, including "industrial extension agents." Training programs for entrepreneurs have been organized, especially in management, marketing and accounting. Entrepreneurs generally need more help in the nature of business as an organization and how the organization fits into the system than in the use of machines. There is already a great deal of artisan-type skill in the hinterlands of the developing countries that can be organized for development.

Perhaps the best example of how governments can assist small industries is provided by Japan.[18] Responsible for policy formulation and supervision is the Smaller Enterprise Agency of the Ministry of International Trade and Industry. Local administrations provide managerial and technical assistance—an "industrial extension service"—and operate special industry institutes and administer loans for equipment modernization. Private industry advice on specific management problems is provided by Small Business Consulting Offices, subsidized by the government.

A wide range of advisory services has now grown up in the private sector, though these are more the result of progress than initial cause. The quality of both public and private services is maintained through auditing by a central agency and through training courses at the government sponsored Japan Productivity Center. Government advisory services, operated out of 300 research and training institutes, center around a diagnostic technique to identify improvements that can be made without significant capital expenditures. In the 1950s, these services were generally provided for individual firms, but this proved to be too expensive because of the very small size of many of the firms. As a result, group diagnoses and "self-education" diagnoses are being used increasingly in order to keep costs reasonable.

A second key element in the success of small industries was the establishment of service cooperatives. By 1959, these numbered 25,000. Their function is to achieve economies of scale by group organization of "production, fabrication, sales, purchasing, transportation, storage, borrowing, and education and information." These cooperatives also help small businesses in bargaining with large firms, for whom a high proportion of the small plants act as subcontractors. Loans for the service cooperatives are provided by a government-sponsored bank.

The government role in helping to finance small industries has been limited to some loans for equipment. Rather, reliance for capital has been placed on a combination of bank-financing for small industries and reinvestment of profits. Interest rates reflected the scarcity of capital: in the 1950s the typical rate on loans for equipment under the government's Small Business Finance Corporation was 9.3 percent. Since private lending to small industries was profitable, the Corporation was only responsible for about 3 percent of total small business loans in 1959—further evidence that a financial system for small producers need not be a permanent drain on the public treasury.

Nevertheless, the emphasis on government assistance in research and management training of myriads of small producers as opposed to trying to play a much larger role in finance seems to have paid off. Small-scale industry is, in general viable, and in recent years has even been suffering from an excess of competition.[19] Many small firms have grown into industrial giants, among them Sony, Honda, and Mitsubishi.

In sharp contrast to the Japanese record, most developing countries have not created the services needed for small industry development. They have not set up large numbers of field offices needed to make these services conveniently available to small producers in market towns and small cities. Most countries have not tried to organize the nation-wide system of capital formation which is needed for small industry development and which should be increasingly financed through private savings and reinvested profits.

The need for industries in rural areas has been recognized in some countries. Some governments have tried to stimulate investment in existing rural urban centers by the organization of "industrial estates." A common method is for the government to purchase land, build factory space and access roads, and install utilities. The government may also provide maintenance facilities. The factory space is then leased or sold to private manufacturers.

However, the record of rural industries is mixed. In the modernizing countries, rural industries are thriving. By contrast, India is an example of a country that has committed two mistakes that must be avoided in developing rural industries—putting city factories in rural areas and failing to integrate rural industries with agriculture.

At one point in the mid-60s, India had 997 "regulated agricultural markets" organized to stabilize prices and introduce quality standards and grading among farmers in the local community. There were 325 industrial estates. Even though the one is a natural complement of the other, only 82 of the 325 estates were in the same towns as the regulated agricultural markets.[20]

Further, many of the factories set up in the estates represented the relocation of city-oriented factories rather than the kind of factories needed to integrate a local urban center with its rural hinterland. Factories in these estates were producing or assembling such things as radios, circuit breakers, gears and gear boxes, nitric acid, and steel furniture. Most of these products can be manufactured more cheaply in the major engineering centers of Bombay, Calcutta, Madras, and

Delhi. In addition, transportation costs were inflated because many of the raw materials were shipped from the big cities to the rural town for production, and then shipped back to the big cities because the market for these products is in cities, not small towns and villages. Because these are the wrong factories in the wrong place production costs are inflated. In a detailed study of four of the estates, it was found that in light engineering factories the amount of capital invested per worker was 2-1/2 to 3-1/2 times as much as in Delhi engineering industries of comparable size! Planners had assumed that because these factories were located in rural areas they would use less capital and create more jobs than factories in the big cities. In fact, the reverse was true.[21]

The Rural Consumer Market

Turning now to the rural consumer market, the first thing to be said is that it is very different from the big city consumer market in both the type of goods consumers want and the amount of capital needed to produce them. There is only a little exaggeration involved in saying that the products that North Americans and Europeans think of as "consumer goods" have become international taste—for the rich. These products require relatively capital-intensive manufacturing processes anywhere in the world. And their manufacture in the developing countries requires substantial foreign exchange because not only the production machines but also many of the raw materials and sometimes components must be imported. Economists tend to frown on rapid increases in consumption because they think of consumption in these terms.

However, "the basic goods which are widely purchased by those on low incomes—essentially food and rather simple manufactures like clothing and footwear are precisely the goods which are produced with techniques considerably more labour intensive than those used in the production of the goods demanded by the rich."[22] This quotation happens to be about Colombia, but the point applies in other parts of the world as well.

The same point also applies to construction as well as to consumer goods. In metropolis, construction tends to be a copy of European and North American building methods and designs, and usually requires the import of materials, construction machinery and furnishings. However, improvements in construction for the lower income groups can be based on local materials, equipment, and techniques which are labor-intensive and capital-saving.

It is futile and expensive to try to industrialize the hinterland with city-type factories and products. Agricultural and rural industrial and market development must advance together. Rural industry does not prosper from an uneconomic relocation of city-type factories but from rising agricultural productivity and farm incomes. It may well be that doubling and trebling productivity on five acre farms, not building steel mills, is the fastest way to create jobs in factories.

In Taiwan, "during the second half of the 1950s, the industrial sector responded by turning to the market offered by accelerated modernization of agriculture."[23] The acceleration of exports by Taiwan from $90 million to $1 billion in 18 years began with processed agricultural products.

A large proportion of the agro-industries and rural consumer goods industries in Taiwan are small, notably those located in market towns and small cities. They tend to employ a great deal of manpower and use rather few machines. Nine-tenths of Taiwan's factories are perhaps more aptly described as "shops," since they employ 10 or fewer workers.[24]

Table 6-2 shows that the capital cost of increasing production in small factories in Taiwan is very much lower than in the city-oriented big factories. Further, the high proportion of total production costs that are paid out in wages in labor-intensive industries stimulates consumer demand, especially in rural areas.

Some Evidence in Support of
Industrial Decentralization

Tables 6-3 and 6-4 are a rough measure of the effect of industrial decentralization on the location of employment and hence the population. Table 6-3 compares the proportion of the population living in metropolis with the proportion of factory jobs located in metropolis. This table shows that the number of factory jobs in metropolis is way out of proportion to the number of people living in metropolis in the dual economy countries, but not in Taiwan and Puerto Rico. Typically, in the smaller countries 1/2 or more of the factory jobs are located in just one city—the capital. In Brazil half the jobs are located in just two cities—Rio and Sao Paulo. The table is one way of showing why market towns and small cities are way stations en route to metropolis in most countries—the lack of jobs in intermediate urban centers.

Table 6-2
Investment Cost of Increasing Production and Labor's Share of Income, by Factory Size, Taiwan, 1961

Size of Industry by Amount of Investment	Investment Cost of Increasing Output by $1.00	Labor's Share of Income per $1.00
less than $2500	$1.97	74¢
$2500 to $25,000	2.52	72¢
$25,000 to $250,000	3.26	50¢
$250,000 to $2.5 million	3.66	39¢
more than $25 million	4.46	31¢

Source: Hsieh and Lee, *Agricultural Development . . . in Taiwan*, p. 97.

Table 6-3
Factory Employment in Metropolis, 1960s

Country & City	Year	Proportion of the Population Living in Metropolis	Proportion of Factory Jobs in Metropolis
Modernizing Countries			
Taiwan–Taipei	1961	9	16
Puerto Rico–San Juan	1963	25	34
Dual Economy Countries			
Mexico–Mexico City	1960	14	55[a]
Brazil–Rio de Janeiro and Sao Paulo	1969	12	52
Pakistan–Karachi	1961	5	51
Turkey–Istanbul	1963	6	35
Thailand–Bangkok-Thonburi	1963	7	61
Chile–Santiago	1965	35	64[b]
Kenya–Nairobi	1963	3	41
Morocco–Casablanca	1960	8	57
Ivory Coast–Abidjan	1965	8	83

Source: All countries–UN Demographic Yearbook, and: Taiwan–*Census of Commerce and Industry*, Taiwan, 1961; Puerto Rico–*Census of Business*, 1963; Mexico–Staley and Morse, *Modern Small Industry for Developing Countries*, p. 300; Brazil–*Statistical Yearbook*, 1968; Pakistan–*Census*, 1961; Turkey–*Statistical Yearbook*; Thailand–*National Statistical Office*; Chile–United Nations Research Institute for Social Development, *Chile* Case Studies on Information Systems for Regional Development, 2 (Geneva, 1970): 9; Kenya, Morocco, Ivory Coast–W.A. Hance, *Population, Migration, and Urbanization in Africa* (New York: Columbia University Press, 1970), pp. 372, 210, and 326 respectively.

[a]Industrial production rather than employment.

[b]Number of factories rather than jobs. Since the larger factories are located in Santiago the proportion of jobs would be higher than the percentage shown on the table.

In sharp contrast, in Taiwan only 1/6 of the factory jobs are located in Greater Taipei. In Puerto Rico, even though 1/4 of the island's population live in the capital city of San Juan, only 1/3 of manufacturing employment is located there. The figures for Taiwan and Puerto Rico are evidence, if evidence is needed, that industrial decentralization is possible when governments are willing to think of traditional small producers as potential modern producers, rather than as inefficient handworkers who will gradually disappear as modernization advances.

Table 6-4 is a somewhat better measure of industrial concentration and dispersion since it includes regional cities as well as the capital. Only two countries are shown–Taiwan and Colombia. Table 6-4 is another illustration of the enormous deficiencies in the type of statistical information that is needed to carry out the policies being discussed in this book. Countries ought to know the loca-

Table 6-4
Distribution of Industrial Employment between Large Cities and Rural Towns—Taiwan, 1961 and Colombia, 1964

	Taiwan	Colombia
Proportion of Population Living in Capital Plus Regional Cities	22%	21%
Proportion of Industrial Jobs in Capital Plus Regional Cities	34%	75%
Ratio of Industrial Jobs to the Population Living Outside of Capital Plus Regional Cities	1 Job per 19 People or 1 Job per 3 Families	1 Job per 49 People or 1 Job per 8 Families

Note: The major cities on which the calculations on the first two lines are: Taiwan-Taipei, Kaohsiung, Tainan, Taichung, Keelung. Colombia-Bogota, Cali, Medellin, Barranquilla.

Source: Taiwan—Derived from *Census of Industry and Commerce, Taiwan 1961*, UN Demographic Yearbook, 1963; *Statistical Abstract of the Republic of China* [Taiwan]: (Taipei; Directorate-General of Budgets, Accounts, and Statistics, 1962); Colombia—Derived from ILO, *Towards Full Employment*, (Geneva: ILO, 1970), p. 97, and UN Demographic Yearbook, 1964.

tion of industrial jobs by urban centers of different size. Such information should be internationally available through the statistical yearbooks which most countries now publish. In fact, very few countries know where industrial jobs are located. And several countries which collect and publish such data do not always summarize it in a usable way. Israel and Yugoslavia are two examples and hence are not included on this table.

To return to table 6-4: it shows both the enormous concentration of industrial jobs in the four major cities of Colombia and the effect of this concentration on the rest of the population in contrast to the geographic dispersal of Taiwan.

In Taiwan, outside of the big cities there is one industrial job for every third family; in Colombia there is one industrial job for every eighth family. This 1 to 3 ratio for Taiwan is a clue to the importance of industry in agricultural development.

In addition to these tables, we can also cite prewar Japan as an outstanding example of industrial decentralization and rural-urban integration. In 1930, six decades after the beginning of modernization of the country, 2/3 of those employed in manufacturing and construction still lived in towns with fewer than 30,000, or in villages. Half of the workers employed in commerce and transport worked in market towns and small cities. More than half the adult members of farm families had some nonagricultural jobs. For 1/4 of the farm families industry actually exceeded agriculture as a source of income.[25]

A second way of getting some notion of the beneficial effects of industrial

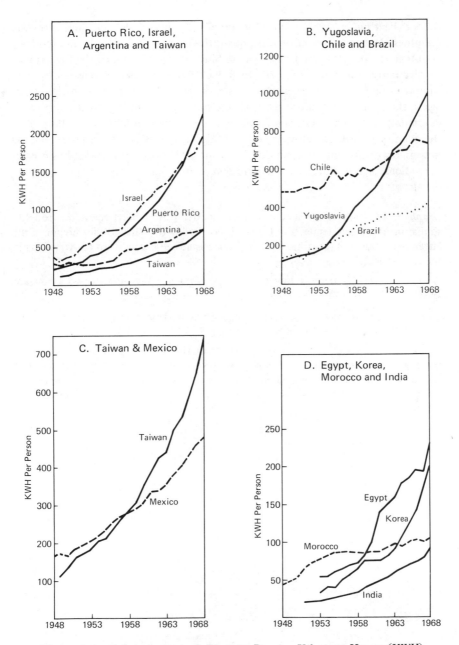

Figure 6-1. Consumption of Electric Power: Kilowatt Hours (KWH) per Person. Source: UN, *World Energy Supplies*, Statistical Papers, Series J, Numbers 1-12.

decentralization is the consumption of electric power. In the dual economy countries electricity is used in large quantities in metropolis. In the modernizing countries electricity is used everywhere. Since industry is much the biggest user of electricity—generally from 2/3 to 3/4 of the total market—electricity consumption ought to be rising much faster in the modernizing countries. Once again, the state of internationally available statistics is limiting. At the very least, consumption in metropolis should be separated from consumption in the rest of the country in order to show the effect of decentralization on the use of electric power. Even this simple separation is not possible. The only available statistics are national totals. But even these are illuminating, as the four graphs of figure 6-1 show:

Graph A. In 1948 the consumption of electric power per person was roughly similar in Argentina, Israel, and Puerto Rico. Today it is three times higher in the latter two than in Argentina. Even Taiwan has already caught up to Argentina in the use of electricity.

Graph B. Starting from a low base, Yugoslavia has far outstripped Chile and Brazil in electric power consumption.

Graph C. This is one of several comparisons in this book which shows the superiority of modernizing Taiwan as compared to dual society Mexico.

Graph D. At a much lower income level than the countries shown in the other three graphs, this graph is perhaps a better comparison of growth rates than actual consumption. The use of electricity in all four countries is still low by any modern standard, but it is rising much faster in Korea and Egypt than in India and Morocco.

7

The Significance of Non-Formal Education

During the period that the great mass of the people are being organized into the society, nonformal education programs need to be organized on a grand scale if people are to acquire the confidence, skills, and knowledge needed to become modern managers and producers.

What is needed in the countries is a nationwide knowledge system. A part of such a system is the formal school structure, which has been the principal object of "educational development" thus far. But people learn from experience as well as from textbooks. It is not sufficient for a farmer to be told by a teacher that fertilizer will increase his output. He must learn how to use particular kinds of fertilizer on his own land. It is not sufficient for a local leader to take a course in leadership training or how to conduct meetings. He must learn how to handle the changing pattern of human relationships inherent in development by helping to manage the modernizing local government or farmer cooperative or other local organization in which he holds a leadership position.

In most developing countries today formal education is not designed to teach people how to use knowledge (discussed further on). This situation must be changed, but modifying attitudes about the nature and purposes of an educational system is a lengthy process.

Living and learning must be combined now if people are to learn how to manage their own situations and use modern technology. A part of this combination is a diversity of training programs, organized outside the formal school system and often called "nonformal education."

Especially in the beginning, nonformal training programs are the only way in which the mass of marginal people can be involved quickly in a nationwide knowledge system, indeed, can help to build such a system. In many countries there is such a shortage of teachers, teaching materials, schools, and money to pay for them, that it may be decades before even primary education becomes universal. Millions of children will be left out of development if the formal school system is the only operational educational system. Similarly, millions of illiterates who are already in their late teens or older will be left out of development if primary reliance is placed on the formal school system to educate the population for development. Further, it is adults, not children, who control a country's production facilities. They own the farms, the artisan, craft, retail, personal service, and repair shops. They also work in the big factories. If training is to influence production and investment decisions quickly, then training programs must be aimed at those who are making these decisions today. Increasing

121

the skill level of an entire society can only be achieved by using nonformal training programs to help people become more productive in their present occupations. While the capacity of the formal education system to train people for development, especially at the higher levels, will gradually be expanded, the need for nonformal training never really ends.

But perhaps the more important reason for emphasizing nonformal education derives from the nature of the traditional formal system and the need to use nonformal training as one way of inducing change in the formal classroom so that the acquisition of knowledge will be related to people's daily lives.

The Separation of Education
and Development

An educational system is one of the major institutions through which a people preserve and transmit the culture and values of their society. Educators do and should regard themselves as guardians as well as transmitters of the ancestral heritage. Today, that heritage seems to be under attack. Development, by definition, is a form of disruption as well as creation. And perhaps it disrupts most of all in the early stages when people are just beginning to understand the values of the world of modern technology but are still uncertain which of the values of their traditional world should or can endure. In particular, the notion of using the educational system to teach the mass of the people the nature and use of technology, that is, job training, is contrary to the traditional purpose of education in Third World countries.

Traditionally, to be educated was to escape from mere technology, to be above and separate from the world in which work is done with the hands. The proportion of people who were educated was very much lower than it is today and their education was nontechnological. Not to need to use technology was one of the virtues of the privileged. To need to use technology was an affliction of poverty. The lore of nature technology which exists in traditional societies was not a proper subject for the school room. Not even the most elementary academic subjects of literacy and simple arithmetic were considered necessary for the subsistence farmer or the artisan. It was simply assumed that the masses who needed to apply the lore of nature would teach each other and their children the knowledge needed for their survival. They would teach this knowledge in their own way, but not in the school room.

In Taiwan today, teenage boys attend vocational agricultural schools in order to become scientific farmers. This is the result of Taiwan's progress, not the cause. The more common attitude in the poor countries toward the value of an education is this: "He leaves agriculture altogether, because cultivation, or in fact any kind of manual work in the rural context, is considered *totally incompatible* with education. The result is that the spread of literacy among the peasant classes helps to improve neither the techniques of cultivation nor agricultural production. . . . Instead of being utilized to improve agriculture, education is looked upon as an avenue of escape from it."[1] The "he" in this quotation is generally a teenage boy who has completed the primary level. "A boy who has been to school up to the seventh or eighth class and who in the company of his friends sees his father working in the field, will tell his friends, 'he is not my father,' he feels so ashamed of him."[2]

The restriction of education to a few was one of the ways in which the elite who ruled kept the rest of the people in their place. In any society, the illiterate and the uneducated do not gain access. Given a tradition in which education is a way of increasing the distance between social classes and in which dirty hands work is considered demeaning and lower class, it is not surprising that the rapid expansion of enrollment in recent decades is not producing the kind of trained manpower required for development. Of the central problem of education, "keeping knowledge alive," Alfred North Whitehead wrote: "In training a child to activity of thought, above all things we [teachers] must beware of what I will call 'inert ideas'—that is to say, ideas that are merely received into the mind without being utilized, or tested, or thrown into new combinations. . . .

"Every intellectual revolution which has stirred humanity into greatness has been a passionate protest against inert ideas."[a]

Education in the developing countries consists largely of rote memorization, even though the idea of development is a "passionate protest" against the "inert idea" of a stagnant society. Development ought to stir the educational systems of the developing countries into greatness. Much of the material which students memorize has little relevance to their lives—it is "inert." Where foreign textbooks are used students do not even memorize material about their own countries. As one African official expressed the point in explaining the need to Africanize the curriculum, he did not want to educate "children who can write the fables of La Fontaine but know nothing of Africa."

Students are not trained to "activity of thought"; they are not trained to "utilize" or "test" or "throw into new combinations" the ideas they receive, but to memorize them for the purpose of recording them on the examination papers. The curriculum is prescribed in detail by government education officials. Better teachers may try to add "other ideas" to this prescribed curriculum. But in a rigid system the students have no incentive to study ideas which will not be included in the examination. Indeed, there are cases on record in which students have protested successfully against the presentation of "other" ideas because they were not a part of the examination. It is almost as if the boundaries of useful knowledge can be determined by governments, and knowledge which is not recognized officially is not worthy of study, or even memorization.

The problem of education in rural communities is further compounded be-

---

[a]This, and the several quotations which follow are from his essay, *The Aims of Education*. Mentor Edition, New York, 1949, pp. 13-27.

cause the "inert knowledge" memorized in village classrooms is prepared almost entirely by city people who have little knowledge, and often little empathy, with village life and agriculture.

Finally, in the rush for expansion, governments have multiplied the existing courses in arts, sciences, and the law at both the higher secondary and university level. They are producing large numbers of graduates with a general education, but without the specialized knowledge in some field of technology the nation requires and with which the student can get a job. Those countries which are producing more graduates than can be employed are creating one of the most unnecessary and destabilizing problems of development—masses of educated unemployed.

Not only is much education in the Third World not useful for development, too often the wrong kind of people are being trained for jobs that need to be done. Both problems afflict the technical and vocational institutes which countries are establishing to meet the need for middle level manpower.

First of all, the notion of using the educational system for job training seems like an attack on all the nonutilitarian values of education which educators cherish most of all, and at a time when these values are in transition. If people are to be given job training in the formal school system, then, educators argue, such training should be subordinated to the concepts and methods of a general education. The educator wants to teach a student of automobile mechanics the theory of hydraulics. What the developing countries need is a mechanic who can change the brake linings whether or not he understands the theory of a hydraulic system. And, when the method of learning continues to be rote memorization, the student does not learn how to think about and use the theory of hydraulics. He simply memorizes a textbook description of the theory.

Further, the students who are eligible to attend these technical and vocational schools are not the people who are willing to do dirty hands work. They do not want to change the brake linings even if they do know how to do it. These institutes are normally located at the middle or higher secondary level of the school. Those who are eligible to enroll must first of all complete a five or six year primary schooling and perhaps also several years of lower secondary schooling. In most countries the proportion of children of secondary school age who are actually in school is very low, usually less than a fifth and in some countries only several percent. These small numbers come from the higher social classes where the disdain for manual labor is most deeply-rooted. Their ambition is to get a college degree—a piece of paper—not to learn a job. For many of the students in these institutes, technical or vocational training is a last resort which they feel obliged to accept if (a) they cannot gain admission to a university, if (b) they fail the examinations in secondary school, or if (c) they do not have enough money for a three or four year university course but can afford to enroll in the much shorter institute courses. Those who become eligible for technical and vocational institutes are those least willing to do dirty hands work, while those who are willing to work do not become eligible because so few of them ever attain the secondary level of school.

In the preceding chapter we described briefly the development of pump manufacturing in the small cities of Pakistan. Generally speaking, the owners of these factories might be described as literate, but not educated. On the average, they completed the primary level and attended secondary school for several years but did not complete this level. Most of them would not have been eligible for the technical institutes established in recent years. Their family job tradition is predominantly blacksmithing, carpentry, and masonry. Most had had some previous experience with simple engineering work, usually through the traditional apprenticeship system. Only several of the more than 100 owners have attended the government vocational school. "None were making more than minimal use of their training."[3]

Similarly, the owners are not hiring the graduates of the technical and vocational institutes: "the polytechnic graduates tried as supervisors worked out unsatisfactorily because of their lack of a good practical knowledge of the trade."[4]

Traditions which involve the basic values of a society, as does educational tradition, are not changed quickly or easily, and not without some conception and confidence in what is to become the new tradition. Education is first of all a matter of teaching a child what it means to be a Canadian or a Brazilian, a Muslim or a Hindu, a Westerner or an African. Other benefits which a society obtains from its educational system, one of which is a supply of skilled manpower, are secondary to this most basic function of education. When this meaning is undergoing change, the educator is uncertain what to teach, especially if the changes are far-reaching. Hence, even in the modernizing countries (here including Western Europe and North America) education tends to be a laggard of development.

It may seem logical, then, to assert that in the dual society countries the prospect of educational reform is remote. The system of rote memorization of "inert knowledge" is, in fact, well suited to a society in which the dominant groups do not want the mass of the people to become problem-solvers and investors. It permits a rapid expansion of school enrollment in rather the same way that Traditional Community Development produces roads and buildings, but it reduces to a minimum the utility of education. Many of those who have it do not know how to use it.

But in education, as in other fields, the actual situation is more complex and less clear-cut than the simple distinction between dual and modernizing societies which we are using to explain the fundamental nature of Third World problems. There are effective training programs in dual society countries, as we shall see later, which are a necessary part of a national knowledge system. They tend to be nonformal rather than a part of the formal school system. They tend to appear first as a way of training the manpower needed for rapid industrialization. Hence, they are mostly urban, not rural. This is partly because trades training institutes around the world tend to be associated with urban jobs, partly because reaching the millions of small farmers requires an unusual approach. To the latter we shall turn first.

Organizing a Training-Knowledge-Communications System

In Western Europe and North America, nonformal education is commonly regarded as either apprenticeship or a specific training course, set up outside the formal school system and taken primarily for the purpose of getting a better job. In the Third World we need a much broader definition. In our part of the world there already exists a combination knowledge-communications-production system in which the graduates of trade, business, and similar schools can find a job. In the Third World this system hardly exists outside of the big cities. In the cities there are already large numbers of vocational training schools and apprenticeship systems, both public and private, similar to those with which we are familiar. We shall return to these programs later.

In rural areas, however, a system to develop, record, communicate, apply and preserve the knowledge which is needed for development barely exists. By now such a system has been organized in enough different places around the world that its principles can be identified, assuming at this point, that the government wants its people to participate in development.

In essence, such a system is the bridge between the traditional knowledge system based on the lore of nature and a modern knowledge system based on applied science. It is organized by using a nonformal training program for villagers as a vehicle for building up the rest of the system. Such a program will be initiated and managed by outsiders, almost certainly the government because there is no other alternative, at least in the early stages of development. The managers will be professionally and technically trained staff in agriculture, engineering, medicine, education, accounting, and other fields. They will work above the level of the individual village—in the local government, cooperatives, and other modernizing institutions discussed earlier. They will teach, supervise, and inspect, but they will not do.

The key to organizing this training-knowledge-communications system is to use the proven principle of extension to combine a handful of trained individuals with the great mass of untrained people. The extension agent is the villager himself, not an outsider trained by the government. Extension is needed not just in agriculture but in a variety of fields. The villager-extension agent, again not the government, is the individual who organizes and mobilizes his fellow villagers for development.

Such training programs must, of course, begin at the villagers' present knowledge level, which is to say, in most countries, the lore of nature. That villagers have learned the lore of nature in intimate detail, that, indeed, it is the application of this knowledge which keeps them alive, should be taken as evidence that they can learn how to apply modern scientific knowledge. The modernizing governments have, in fact, recognized that the uneducated are not always unwise, the illiterate are not always ignorant.

The villagers themselves should select those who will serve as their agents. Some of them will be managers of the village organizational units which are members of the county and township organizations—for example, the village development committee which works with the township government in Taiwan or the village cooperative societies which are federated at the county level in Comilla, Bangladesh. Larger numbers of village agents will be needed for the technical tasks—agriculture, bookkeeping, literacy programs, sanitation, child care, youth clubs, and so on. It is the need for designated individuals to take charge of the enormous number of specific tasks of development that makes it possible to create more leadership positions than there are traditional leaders to fill them—the fifth principle of organizing people discussed in chapter 2.

The training programs for village extension agents should emphasize the concepts, organization, and management of the new local institutions, and their linkages with the regional and national levels rather than the technical aspects of development. Agricultural extension in Taiwan emphasizes "planning, management, evaluation, marketing, and other considerations in agricultural economics,"[5] that is, how a farmer can maximize his income in the national agricultural system.

At Comilla County the village society is supposed to meet weekly.[b] The discussions at these meetings revolve around the organization and its work—maintaining organizational discipline, standards of individual performance, developing work plans, and assigning specific jobs to members. "However, the weekly meeting is seldom used as a forum for imparting knowledge and skills in improved [agricultural] practices."[6]

This emphasis on institutions rather than technology is almost the reverse of the emphasis of most underdeveloped governments and development assistance agencies. The latter have been stressing technology. However, the villagers seem to understand that part of "the evolution of a different art of living and working together" is a matter of "institutional development" (to use the bureaucratic phrase). For example, organizational discipline is needed to maintain the credit rating of the township or county cooperative. The villagers must learn both how to apply this kind of discipline among themselves (a function of the local financial institutions of the national economy) and why the credit rating of their local cooperative is important (a function of the regional or national financial institutions of the national economy). Hence, the need to emphasize in training programs the nature, management, and discipline of "the system."

Granting that training will be based on knowledge which originates in the out-

---

[b]In fact, the societies meet, on average, about three times a month.

side world—such as agricultural science, engineering, or how to run meetings—the training programs should be based on the day-to-day problems encountered by the villagers as they try to apply this outside knowledge in their own communities. It is the combination of this type of training for the villager-agent and meetings held by the agents in their villages that make problem-solving a part of the routine activities of daily life.

Further, whatever the villagers do must be recorded. Traditionally, villagers rely on their memories. (The stylistic embellishments added through generations of recitation accounts for the poetic and picturesque quality of village speech in contrast to the descriptive, precise but rather flat quality of our technological and organizational language). But the modern world is much too complicated for people to rely on their memories. There are, of course, many uses of written records, both at the local level and at high levels. The farmer must not only learn how different kinds and quantities of fertilizer affects the crops he grows on his own fields, but how to compare the costs of fertilizer and other possible investments with probable gains. The records of demonstration plots in local areas are an important part of the data base for agricultural information programs. They are also needed by agricultural scientists if they are to solve the technical problems of the farmers of their own country. And so forth, for every subject of development.

The kind of training programs being discussed here must be continuous. The pattern for most of the village agents at Comilla County is a weekly training program at county headquarters followed by a meeting, a discussion group, a demonstration, whatever is appropriate, in the village. From the beginning the villagers are taught that discovering, applying, and communicating knowledge is a never-ending process.

Finally, those who set about organizing this type of training-knowledge-communications system must understand that a main purpose of the formal local organization is to set in motion those informal processes of communication and personal relationships that make an organization come alive. "Communication is part and parcel of social relations. Horizontal communication far exceeds vertical communication. Agricultural-extension agencies pass very little information from their high offices in towns and cities down to the farmers in the villages. The effective extension work is done personally in the villages where the farmers or farm women gather. . . . The results of many information diffusion researches show that farmers get most information through their neighbors, friends, fellow-farmers."[7] This is Taiwan. But the same point—the importance of horizontal communications in the nonofficial circuit—has been found in information diffusion studies in many countries around the world, including our own.

At the end of the sixth year of the Comilla County program, some 11,000 villagers were involved in the type of training-knowledge-communications program described above (out of an adult population of some 75,000). The kinds of people trained are listed below. Although the list is a bit long, it is included to illustrate how knowledge can be accumulated in a variety of fields, how much training can be organized in a community which was, in the beginning, 80 percent illiterate. Hardly any of those who were literate were "educated" in any modern sense.

The training programs for villagers at Comilla cover: officers of the village cooperatives, agricultural extension agents, bookkeepers and accountants, village "doctors," village midwives (almost all of them illiterate), primary school principals and teachers, research enumerators, family planning workers, officers of the women's and youth organizations, councilors and employees of the local government, chairman and members of the "project committees" in charge of building farm-to-market roads and simple irrigation and drainage systems, and literacy teachers.

By subject there were also courses in home sanitation, spinning and sewing, operation and maintenance of mechanical farm equipment, first aid, forestry, maternal and child health, silk-screen printing, and gardening and poultry (programs such as the latter two are the only way the problem of malnutrition can ever be solved).

In this type of training program, it is assumed that job differentiation will gradually increase: as full-time specialists can be trained in large numbers in vocational, technical and college level institutions; as increasingly complex and sophisticated knowledge is needed for "the next steps"; and as villagers become so busy that they no longer have the time to be part-time, elementary level technicians. In Taiwan, for example, farmers now work three or four times as many hours per year as farmers at Comilla prior to 1960. They take the time to manage their local organizations and carry on some demonstrations. However, they rely on full-time technical staff employed by government, the cooperatives, and private business to carry out many specific tasks which farmers at Comilla, at a lower technological level, are still doing themselves on a part-time basis.

This is to say that where there has not yet been much development, low-level, nonformal training, carried out in the context of modernizing institutions, is one of the keys to getting people involved in development, and a way for people gradually to move out of the low productivity knowledge base of the lore of nature and into the high productivity knowledge base of modern science. In Taiwan, applied science has made farming a respectable occupation. Teenage boys are willing to attend vocational agricultural high school to learn how to be farmers. In most developing countries farming is still associated with the static productivity world of tradition, the world that is to be left behind. It is not a respectable occupation. This is why teenage boys who have only a primary education believe they have learned how not to become farmers. "The benefits of [formal] training become apparent *after* the fact of agricultural development, not before."[8] To this should be added the almost self-evident point that when parents understand it is more important for their children to go to school than to help do the work, then they will insist that education be made more relevant.

Problems of the Urban Poor

The kind of training-knowledge-communications system, here described, needs to be created primarily in rural areas—villages and market towns. In the cities much of it already exists, even in the shanty towns of metropolis. The common problem in the cities is that there are two systems, the official system managed by those who rule and the system the poor people have organized for themselves. Usually the government does not recognize the latter's existence.

The word "slum" is more an attitude of mind than a description of the physical characteristics of an urban community. The word implies a fatalistic acceptance of poverty, a hopeless view of the future. The shabby appearance of the shanty towns in the Third World can be deceptive. Often the people who live in these communities are highly organized. They are trying to participate in development.

In Latin America, for example, there are low-income urban communities that organize unofficial local governments, elect their own officers, collect taxes, build streets, provide water supplies and sewerage systems, organize housing projects and primary schools, operate employment services and also unofficial arbitration tribunals to resolve community disputes.[9] These communities seem shabby and crowded because incomes are low, because of the employment problem, and because they cannot get sufficient help from governments since they are "unofficial." But it is self-evident that people who can organize their own community and carry out their own development projects have learned how to acquire, use, communicate, and preserve knowledge; and also that they have also acquired considerable skill in managing their own organizations. Their problem is that they belong to the unseen part of the dual society.

To some extent, however, the gap between the two groups in the cities is being bridged through trades training institutes organized outside the formal education system. Apprenticeship training has been expanding rapidly, but not fast enough to meet the demand for technical and vocational skills. Hence, many countries are establishing trades training institutes similar to those which are common in Europe and North America for both initial training and upgrading the skills of those already working.

One of the best of these is in Colombia, the National Apprenticeship Service, generally known by its Spanish acronym, SENA. "It organizes and operates a vast array of training programs for workers in the industrial, commercial, agricultural, animal husbandry, mining, hotel and catering, as well as medical services (nurses) and even vocational training in the military.[10] SENA is financed by a 2 percent payroll tax.

SENA offers a wide range of training programs from foreman to supervisory courses to short courses for semiskilled workers, currently at a rate exceeding 300,000 per year. It also operates a consulting business for firms that run their own training programs. It operates in small towns, by using mobile training units, as well as in the large cities. The training programs are based on manpower surveys and consultations with employers about the skills they need.

This type of nonformal skills training is spreading rapidly throughout Latin America and Africa, though rather more slowly in Asia where vocational training is too often located in secondary schools. Usually training institutes are financed from the government budget. More countries should emulate Colombia's financial discipline by requiring employers to help pay the costs of training their work force.

For urban industrialists these nonformal programs are a source of trained manpower, though even in these programs training is not always as practical as it should be. By involving employers in the direction of skills training programs, as does Tanzania through the National Industrial Training Council, then such training can be tied to the kind of jobs that are being created. In most countries, however, this kind of close working relationship between government and private groups is still uncommon.

Trades training schools, in which social origin is ignored and in which traditional academic qualifications are discarded, are the kind of schools the poor can be expected to attend. They offer the opportunity of obtaining security of income in a manner the downtrodden can understand and accept. They offer the only hope of meeting, with some reasonable degree of speed, the enormous requirements for skilled manpower in the developing countries. Hence, they are a necessary part of a nationwide knowledge system.

However, these skills training programs pertain only to "economic development." As long as the neighborhood communities in which the urban poor live continue to be regarded as "unofficial," then a training-knowledge-communications system for the cities, one that covers both economic and noneconomic activities, will be incomplete.

The problem is that the existing socializing institutions—schools, the local government, community centers, radio stations, and others—are geared in content and style to the interests, problems, and living modes of the elites. They seem somewhat remote from the daily activities of the poor. For example, education programs are based on theory and the higher levels of the formal school system. They are presented in the "classical" language of the upper classes. What the poor need is practical programs presented in the more colloquial language which they speak.

On the other hand, many of the socializing institutions which the people trust and use are ones they have organized themselves, without official support and recognition. These institutions not only need to be recognized by governments as institutions through which they can reach their citizens; they need to be linked to and receive assistance from regional and national institutions, as discussed in chapter 2.

The Incentive for Literacy

It is self-evident that literacy is a basic element of a nationwide knowledge system. The most important element of a literacy program is not the program itself, but the incentive to become, and remain, literate. When people are able to believe they can improve their lives through their own efforts, when they realize that some newly created opportunity is denied to them by illiteracy, then they will learn how to read, write, and count. According to a survey in one country, people say their principal reason for wanting to become literate is "so that the government officials will no longer be able to cheat us." Specifically, they felt they should be able to read the land tax records as one way of protecting themselves from the traditional petty extortions of land and tax officials who can lie with impunity if people cannot read official records.

Literacy has suffered by being treated by the advocates of universal literacy as a kind of panacea for whatever they conceive to be the ailments of an underdeveloped country. However, marginal people see no reason to be literate. One of the strangest experiences a Westerner can have is to hear a person say that, while he is not sure because he has not tried for a long time, he thinks he has forgotten how to read!

Literacy does not provide access if people are not organized to participate in development. For this reason, there appears to be little relationship between literacy and economic growth. When the Age of Development began, the rate of literacy in the Philippines and some Latin countries was considerably higher than in Taiwan and Korea and is still much higher than in Egypt, or Comilla County, Bangladesh. Argentina and Chile combine exceptionally high literacy rates, by Third World standards, with very low economic growth rates.

When the incentive is present, people will teach each other how to read and write. Some statistics from nineteenth century Britain offer an interesting insight into the relationship between literacy and the expansion of primary schooling.

According to the Newcastle Commission, the percentage of primary age children enrolled in primary schools in Britain in 1861 was around 60 to 65 percent. Average attendance is not known but may have been rather low because of the poor attendance in what were called the "non-inspected" schools, which were then more than half the total number of primary schools. However, the proportion of literacy is estimated at about 75 percent. In the early 1890s, by which time the statistical information is better, enrollment in primary schools was at least 3/4 of the age group and possibly as high as 85 percent. Average attendance was about 2/3. But literacy was 95 percent. Thus, in Britain literacy spread faster than primary education.[11]

Throughout the nineteenth century, no subject outside of politics was more popular among British reformers than education, which first of all meant literacy for the working groups. Literacy courses were popular because ordinary people who had never been to school realized the necessity of literacy in their rapidly industrializing society. People of all ages were able to study reading, writing, and arithmetic in all sorts of places—high schools, trade unions, settlement houses, churches, some trade schools, and elsewhere. In fact, Sunday School began in Britain, before child labor was abolished, as a literacy program for children who worked in factories and mines during the week. In the drive for universal literacy the voluntary associations and local governments organized literacy courses wherever a class could be assembled.

Whether literacy is advancing more rapidly than primary schooling in today's developing countries we have not been able to discover. But the point is worth checking. Quite likely new incentives and opportunities will mean more to illiterates than the adult education courses that have proliferated throughout the Third World in the past two decades and that have not been able to reduce the level of illiteracy significantly.

8

Population and Exports as Evidence

Modernizing Countries and the Population Non-Explosion

Of the various problems of the developing countries none seems so potentially ominous as the "population explosion." When Columbus discovered America, the world's population was doubling every other century. Today it is doubling every third of a century, in some countries at an even faster rate. It is all too easy to conjure up the image of the Malthusian explosion. Just as the employment problem can be managed, so also can the population problem be reduced to manageable proportions. The two problems are, of course, inter-related, since the employment problem will be much easier to solve in the long run if population growth rates decline. At the same time, however, it appears that birth rates decline significantly in the poor countries only when they have managed to achieve a substantial measure of modernization, which, in turn, depends in part on creating enough decent jobs.

In a few countries the birth rate is declining rapidly from the very high rates that seem to be characteristic of traditional societies. The names of these countries will not be repeated here for the reader is now familiar with them. The point is that the personal incentives for voluntary limitation of family size appear to be inherent in modernizing policies, that is, our family planning policy has already been set forth in the seven preceding chapters. If the personal incentives are present, then adults will use the family planning gadgetry that is available now in urban and rural dispensaries throughout the Third World. If, however, the personal incentives are lacking, then the availability of the gadgetry does not mean parents will use it. Those who anticipate a decline in birth rates because the means of control are now widely available are likely to endure the same disappointment as those who assumed small farmers would use fertilizer once it became available at a local warehouse.

The "population explosion" was set off by a rapid decline in death rates without a parallel reduction in birth rates. In the course of this century the death rate has been reduced from 30 or more per thousand living people (usually written as 30 per 1000) to under 20 per 1000 in nearly all of the poor countries and less than 10 per 1000 in a few. Through famine relief and modern techniques of epidemic disease control central governments are able to prevent, or at least mitigate, the effects of catastrophe. That is, the death rate can be reduced by programs which can be carried out without altering the organization of a dual soci-

135

ety and which do not require the voluntary participation of people en masse over an extended period of time. But family limitation is a matter of individual persuasion and privacy, one of the aspects of the life of subsistence which lies beyond the reach of government officials.

"The effective control of fertility requires individual initiative and sustained effort. People who do not really believe that it is possible for them to improve conditions of life for themselves or their children will not undertake a radically new venture or put forth the sustained effort for success in this undertaking. Where hope is weak, contraception will be absent or ineffective."[1]

This quotation assumes that the "classical population curve"[a] is still a valid explanation of trends in birth rates. The concept of the "curve" was developed as an explanation of what appeared to be a paradox in North America and Europe a century ago. At the very same time that rising incomes made it easier for parents to afford the very large families that were traditional, birth rates began to fall. Because they declined—and substantially—we have been spared what is now called the "population explosion."[2]

There are a number of reasons why dual societies have high birth rates. Until very recently, more children meant more labor and hence more food because there was still arable land to be cultivated. And since the young care for the aged more children meant more security in old age. In some societies there is a tradition of pride in large numbers of sons. A father with an "excess" of daughters wanted more children in the hope of having sons. Until very recently the child mortality rate was so very high that parents believed they needed to have 10 babies in order to have 5 grown children.

These attitudes begin to change, though slowly, as the death rate is reduced radically so that parents can believe that most of their children will survive, and as the ideas of development begin to permeate a society and gradually change attitudes toward many things. As new opportunities are created, parents begin to realize that educating children already born is more important than additional children. The same point applies to better medical care, leisure time, better housing, perhaps most of all, the possibility of upward mobility in the social structure. New forms of security are developed so that parents become less dependent on children in old age or times of adversity.

These are some of many possible examples of the definition of development given in the second chapter—"the evolution of a different art of living and work-

---

[a]Also sometimes called the "demographic transition." As explained by demographers, there are four stages:

1. High death and birth rates = low rate of population increase.
2. Declining death rate and high birth rates = high rate of population increase. Most of the Third World is in this stage.
3. Declining death and birth rates = declining rate of population increase. A few Third World countries, as discussed above, are in this stage.
4. Low death and birth rates = low rate of population increase. The developed countries are in this stage.

ing together." Part of that "different art"·is a concept of family which differs significantly from the traditional concept of family in two respects. First, the "extended" family (aunts, uncles, brothers, sisters, cousins, and so forth) declines in importance. Secondly, the "unitary" family (parents and their own children) is small. Thus far in history this change in both the concept and size of family seems to be universal. It has happened in the countries called "developed." It is beginning to happen in the recently successful countries. In Taiwan, for example, the younger generation now favors small families rather than the traditional as many children as possible.[3]

Figure 8-1 suggests that the classical population curve may be as valid today in explaining population trends in the Third World as when it was first used earlier in this century to explain the decline in birth rates in Europe and North America.

Earlier in this book we described Taiwan as a modernizing country and Mexico as the oldest of the dual society countries. The figure shows the birth and death rates for the two countries from 1930 to the present and also the difference between the two which is called the "natural" increase in the population.

For almost two decades there has been a continuous decline in the birth rate in Taiwan. The rate has declined almost one-half from the peak of 1951 and is now down to 25 per 1000.

Further, the decline set in before the advent of that recent addition to development programs, family planning—evidence that the personal incentives inherent in modernizing policies are indeed the key to voluntary limitation of family size.

Finally, the rate is still declining. (For comparison we should note that the birth rate in the Western countries and Japan ranges from 12 to 18 per 1000).

In contrast to Taiwan, the birth rate in Mexico has remained relatively constant at a little more than 40 per 1000 throughout the four decades shown on the figure. The effect of these different trends in birth rates is shown on the "natural" increase chart. The population growth rate in Taiwan is now down to 2 percent. In Mexico the rate continues to be well above 3 percent each year. The reader will also note that the death rate in Taiwan is much lower than in Mexico—evidence of the spread of rural medical services in the former.

For two other modernizing countries, Puerto Rico and Yugoslavia, the trends are similar to those shown on the charts for Taiwan. In Puerto Rico the birth rate declined from 40 per 1000 in the mid-1940s to 25 per 1000 in 1969. The population increase is down to 2 percent each year, as in Taiwan. In Yugoslavia the birth rate has declined from the post-World War II high of 30 per 1000 to 18 per 1000. The rate of increase is only 1 percent each year.

For most of the Third World countries it is not possible to draw the kind of charts shown here. Most dual society governments have been indifferent to the type of information called "vital statistics." Governments have not been gathering and keeping up-to-date, accurate information on the size of their popula-

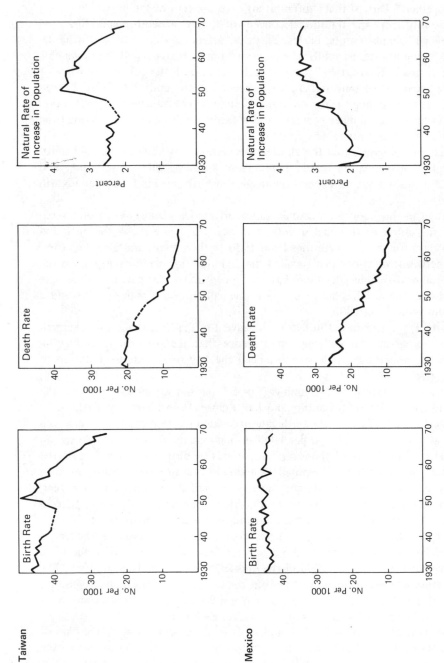

Figure 8–1. The Classical Population Curve. (Statistics are not available for the period of WWII for Taiwan) Source: *UN Demographic Yearbook,* 1948–1969 and UN, *Monthly Bulletin of Statistics,* September, 1971.

tions, the number of babies who are born each year, the number of people who die and the causes of death, and similar matters. This attitude is changing, but the change is recent. In the absence of reliable data much of the demographic information now available is based on sample surveys carried out by professional demographers and statisticians, sponsored primarily by the United Nations.

The birth rate in most of the Third World countries is currently estimated at 35 to 50 per 1000. As far as is known, it has not changed significantly in recent years. Because the death rate has been reduced so much, the population growth rate is very high. As family planning programs spread throughout the underdeveloped world, doubtless the birth rate will be reduced somewhat, just as there has been a modicum of agricultural progress through the years. But the dramatic reduction in birth rates which is needed is not likely to occur without the creation of individual incentives through the modernizing policies discussed in this book. Thus, it may well be that the organization of market towns or viable farmer cooperatives is the first step in reducing birth rates.[4]

The Capacity to Compete

Just as modernizing policies provide incentives for voluntary limitation of family size, so also do these policies enable a country to develop skills and attitudes needed to compete in the international market.[5]

Except for the oil and mineral rich countries (Venezuela, Iran, and so on) only a small number of countries have succeeded in increasing their exports rapidly and continuously to the point where "foreign aid" is no longer needed. These countries are now able to purchase from their own export earnings capital equipment and other imports needed for both investment and consumption. They are the same countries being cited throughout this book as modernizing. By contrast, many other developing countries are still dependent on "foreign aid."

The export performance of selected Third World countries during the past twenty years is shown on figure 8-2.

Two of the modernizing countries, Taiwan and Yugoslavia, are shown in the top section. In both countries exports per capita have risen from around $10 a year in 1950 to more than $70 a year in 1969. Exports have been rising continuously and rapidly in both countries primarily because of their capacity to produce an increasing variety of products which can be exported, that is, diversification of the national production system, and their capacity to break into the market for manufactured products. Their dependence on a handful of low-unit value, mostly unprocessed products is now a thing of the past.

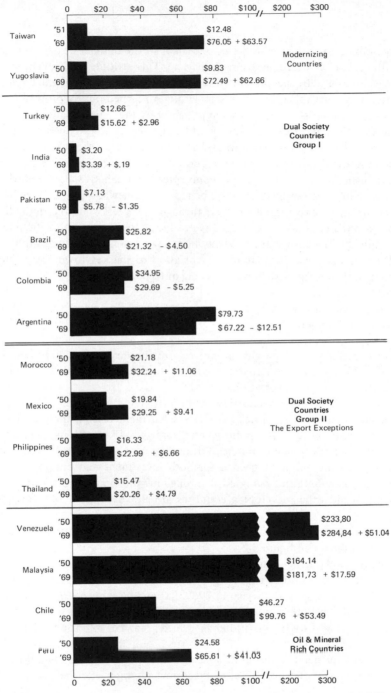

Figure 8-2. Exports Per Capita, Selected Countries, 1950 and 1969.
Source: *UN International Trade Yearbook*, 1951–53, 1969 and *Commodity Trade Statistics*, 1969.

Israel and Puerto Rico also belong in this category, although they are generally considered to be special cases; Israel because it was settled by "developed" people who already knew how to organize a modern society, as did those who migrated from Europe to our own country, Canada, Australia, and New Zealand. Puerto Rico is considered a special case because of its access to the United States' market, obviously an unusual advantage. It is worth saying, however, that although Puerto Rico enjoyed this access from 1898 to 1948, there was little development. The island commonwealth did not somehow float closer to the American continent in 1948. What happened in that year was the installation of a government that adopted the modernizing policies being discussed in this book, enabling Puerto Rico to take advantage of an opportunity that had lain dormant for half a century.

The dual-society countries are divided into two groups on the chart. Those countries which continue to be dependent on a small number of "primary" agricultural products (coffee, tea, cotton, jute, tobacco, and so on) account for nearly all the Third World countries—Group I on the chart. Some of these countries also export modest quantities of mineral ores. The exports of these countries are low unit value, that is, the value of any of these products is relatively low compared to the value of iron ore which is transformed and exported as a bicycle or an engine. World demand for these products has not been rising nearly as rapidly as demand for manufactures. This slow growth of demand has meant that none of these countries has been able to increase exports by more than a few dollars per person in the past two decades. Moreover, in several countries exports per capita have actually declined.

A few Third World countries fall into yet another category, the "Export Exceptions"—the third group of countries shown on the chart. These countries increased enormously the quantity of primary products exported and thereby increased export earnings moderately—from $5 to $10 per person as compared to $60 in Taiwan and Yugoslavia. Thailand has added to her traditional major exports of rice and tin ore two other low unit value agricultural crops—corn and kenaf (a jute-like fibre).

The Philippines has increased export earnings by exporting more sugar, pineapples, logs and some wood products, coconuts, and copper. These few products still accounted for 7/8 of the Philippines' exports in 1968.

The bulk of Morocco's increased export earnings come from the large farm modern agricultural sector and minerals.

Mexico is discussed further on.

The lesson to be drawn from the "Export Exceptions" is clear: the capacity to compete is a manufacturing capacity. The developing countries cannot increase their foreign exchange earnings rapidly or sufficiently by exporting increased quantities of primary products.

The fourth group of countries is evidence, if evidence is needed, that money alone is not the catalyst of development.

It is sometimes said that Taiwan is an exceptional case because of the large amount of American aid—about $150 per person over a 15 year period. Obviously American aid helped Taiwan to a running start. However, the export earnings of the oil, mineral, rubber-rich countries such as Venezuela, Chile, Peru, Malaysia, and the oil-rich states of the Middle East are much higher than the amount of foreign aid countries are receiving. However, their exportable products come mostly from modern enclaves, mines and plantations, that often have little impact on the bulk of the economy or the bulk of the people. With the partial exception of Malaysia, none of these countries has yet achieved an agricultural revolution or adopted an integrated agricultural-industrial-commercial development policy. None of them has achieved a really high rate of sustained economic growth over several decades.

Economists are not agreed on the exact nature of cause and effect in export growth. Rapid export growth is essential for development; yet increasing exports is dependent on development.

Despite this causal dilemma, factors involved in rapid and continuous export growth can be identified, and, in general, can be grouped together as (a) economic and fiscal policies and (b) agro-industrial growth.

The latter comprises the combination of rising agricultural productivity and agricultural-industrial integration discussed in preceding chapters of this book. This strategy of successful rural development not only brings about production increases, some of which can be exported, but also produces an enormous increase in a country's supply of managerial talent, intelligent risk-taking, and technical skills. In the long run, it is these human skills in organizing production and meeting competition that enables a country to compete on the international market. In modernizing countries these skills are no longer concentrated in the big cities and in the government but are distributed throughout the society and the economy. The different levels of the economy are so linked together that the perception of export opportunities is conveyed to the production sections, even to two-acre farmers, thus transforming these opportunities into actual overseas sales.

With regard to economic and fiscal policy, the successful export countries have been characterized as "outward looking." That is, the governments have adopted a set of policies regarding exchange rates, tariffs, import quotas, taxation, credit, product standardization, quality control, and so on, which both help their country's producers compete on the international market and subject them to the discipline of international competition in such things as price, quality control, packaging, reliable delivery dates, and spare parts for equipment. Decentralization, a preference for general policy rather than detailed administrative regulation, and investment in capital-saving, labor-intensive investment in industry are all characteristics of the "outward-looking" countries.

"Inward looking," on the other hand, characterizes policies favoring overvalued exchange rates, high tariffs, import quotas, licensing systems designed to protect domestic industry, and the pursuit of excessively capital-using, labor-saving industries. Such policies seem to go hand in hand with highly centralized governments and detailed administrative regulation of the economy.

Figure 8-3 compares the export success of one modernizing country, Taiwan, with the problems of a dual-society country such as Mexico. Taiwan, as previously explained, is perhaps the best example in recent times of the way in which modernizing policies can transform a subsistence society. Both characteristics of a successful export policy described above, "outward-looking" economic policies and agro-industrial integration will be found in Taiwan. Mexico's economic policy is rather more "outward looking" than many Third World countries. However, as explained above, Mexico has thus far failed to modernize peasant agriculture or to achieve a high measure of agro-industrial integration. This is one reason why industrial production increased only 3 1/2 times in Mexico between 1953 and 1969, but 7 1/2 times in Taiwan.

In both 1951 and 1968 Taiwan earned almost $75 million from three primary products: sugar, rice, and tea. In the first year these low unit value products constituted almost 3/4 of Taiwan's total exports, but in 1968 they were only 9 percent—evidence of the enormous diversification of export products. By 1968 Taiwan was earning $160 million per year ($200 per farm family) from bananas, pineapples, mushrooms, asparagus and other new food exports—evidence of her progress in agriculture. Some 60 percent of total agricultural exports, or $250 million, were processed or manufactured—evidence of the integration of agricultural and industrial development.

In 1951 Taiwan's processed exports were negligible, only $8 million. But in 1968 processed and manufactured exports were no less than $600 million, 3/4 of the total. This is the real measure of Taiwan's progress. Hardly any of these products were manufactured—let alone exported—in 1951. Today Taiwan not only exports textiles and clothing, but textile machinery, plus chemicals, medicines, electronics equipment, plastic products, small-size engines and motors, and a variety of other high-unit value manufactured products.

By contrast, Mexico still depends mainly and excessively on primary products for her commodity export earnings. Total export earnings increased by $790 million between 1950 and 1968, just a little more than the total increase in Taiwan. Yet Mexico has 3 1/2 times as many people, 25 times as much cultivated land, and, like Puerto Rico, lies next door to the largest consumer market in the world—the United States. Indeed, 3/4 of Mexico's exports are purchased by the United States. Mexico also has considerable mineral wealth, Taiwan very little.

Although Mexico would appear to have natural advantages over Taiwan, mostly low unit value, unprocessed exports continued to comprise the largest share, 71 percent, of Mexico's exports in 1968; the share of processed and manufactured exports increased from 7 to only 29 percent between 1951 and 1968.

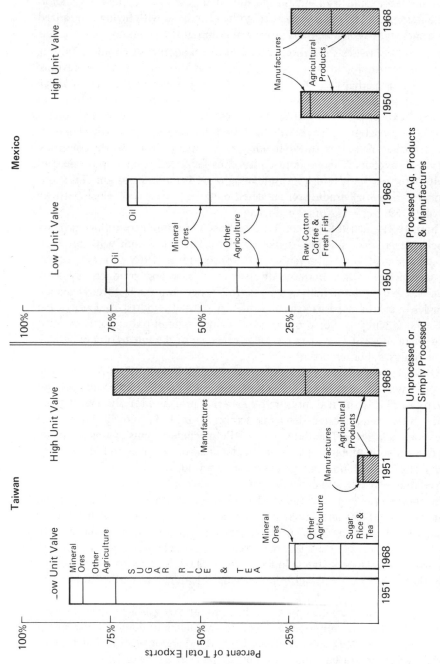

Figure 8–3. Composition of Exports, Taiwan and Mexico, 1950 and 1968. Source: *UN International Trade Yearbook*, 1968 and UN *Commodity Trade Statistics*, 1968.

The increase in food exports was considerable, over $300 million. However, most of these products come from the modern, large-farm sector of Mexican agriculture. Unlike Taiwan, small farmers do not benefit much from export crops. Processed and manufactured exports increased by $200 million, only 1/3 of the increase of the same type of exports from Taiwan, and, on a per capita basis, less than 1/10.

To give one other comparison, in 1969 the export of manufactures by Taiwan and Korea combined was about 3 times as large as from the whole of Latin America (excluding trade between the Latin countries), even though the population and industrial output of the two Asian countries are only 1/8 as much.

Thus, the export record suggests that modernizing policies are the key to what the Third World countries would call economic independence and self-respect, and we would describe as an end to "foreign aid."

The United States and the Developing Countries

The people of the United States today are showing rather little concern over the two and a half billion people in the developing world. This is hardly surprising: The trauma of Indo-China has led to a desire for psychological and physical isolation from the seemingly intractable problems of development, lest continued involvement lead to further misadventure.

At the same time, many of our people have begun to question whether we should try to help faraway places at a time when there are so many dilemmas at home—race, the cities, unemployment, inflation, the search for values. Further, there is a widespread feeling that we may not possess the wisdom to help solve the development problems of countries which are vastly different from our own in culture, religion, and custom. In addition, many in the United States have come to believe that aid has served only to make the rich richer and to prop up corrupt and inefficient governments on the basis of a rather nebulous concept of "national security."

This combination of factors—disenchantment over Vietnam, anxiety about the situation at home, and declining confidence in our ability to help—has eroded the support for constructive policies towards the developing countries.

Why Should Americans Care?

For a number of reasons, it is simply not possible for the United States to divorce itself entirely from the problems of 2/3 of mankind. In the first place, the United States has enshrined in its history and culture a desire to help the less fortunate. The right to "life, liberty, and the pursuit of happiness," in our Declaration of Independence is not limited to the people of the United States but is asserted for "all men." This desire to help the marginal people cannot, of course, be achieved by narrow concentration on self-interest or neoisolationism.

Then there are several points which are related to our national self-interest. The developed countries bought $33 billion worth of imports from the poor countries in 1968, essential commodities such as oil, metals, agricultural products, and low price manufactures that help keep down the cost of living. And, in turn, these amounts earned by the poor countries were used to buy exports from the rich countries. These benefits of international trade would be endangered by continued political turbulence in the Third World. Again, the overseas investment of United States business in the developing countries now totals $20 bil-

147

lion: much of this investment might be threatened by continued uncertainty, frustration, and instability in the countries. At the same time, the people of the United States enjoy the freedom to travel widely in the world, including the poor countries. American retreat into isolationism might lead to curtailment of this freedom.

Finally, and most importantly, there is the question of the sort of world we want our children to grow up in. We must remember that our policies towards the rest of the world will not just affect United States' security or balance of payments over the next year or even the next decade. Rather, they are part of an historical process: they help create an atmosphere and a set of conditions that will have a lasting effect on the relationships between countries and peoples. If present trends continue, the number of people standing on the sidelines watching but not participating in development will multiply severalfold. World Bank President Robert McNamara has expressed this dramatically:

The 'marginal' men, the wretched strugglers for survival on the fringes of farm and city, may already number more than half a billion. By 1980, they will surpass a billion, by 1990 two billion. Can we imagine any human order surviving with so gross a mass of misery piling up at its base?[1]

McNamara's figures are no more than guesses. What is important is the trend he highlights, and the question he asks in the light of that trend. The question really has two aspects. The first is the threat of political instability stemming from inequities in the poor countries boiling over into the international arena, causing dangerous, ambiguous situations which could lead to misjudgments by major powers. Though we do not know enough about the relationship between mass misery and political upheaval, it is plausible to suggest that as communications and ideologies spread, and as the pressures on dual society governments grow, then political instability will increase as misery continues to spread. One reaction to this possibility is for the United States to continue to devote part of its wealth to building a military machine capable of crushing any uprisings that might be considered dangerous to the American national interest before they spill into the international arena. Hopefully, our experience in Indo-China has taught us that neither government by benevolence nor military force is a feasible solution to the human problems of development. Furthermore, the use of an unworkable solution abroad tears at the fabric of our society at home.

This leads to the second and deeper aspect of McNamara's question—what happens to the most powerful nation in the world when it decides to ignore the misery of hundreds of millions of people? Can the United States pursue a deliberate long-term policy of ignoring the fate of the world's poor? How would this affect the conscience of the world's richest nation? And how would our people manage to equate their faith in the possibility of bettering the lot of mankind with inaction? Vast divergences between a nation's ideals and its actions must create tensions and dilemmas within that society. How would these work themselves out?

However, these interests, both humanitarian and more narrow, do not answer the question of how the United States can help in alleviating misery in the world. It is interesting to note that, while arguments over these issues have been aggravated in the last few years, they have a history as old as the aid program. Back in 1950, the New York Times carried the following story from India:

Robert North of Stanford University, after hearing the Asian speaker arraign United States' policies and impugn the motives of the United States, made a statement. . . . A summary of his points follows: 'If the West gives aid it will be feared for its imperialism; if it withholds aid it will be denounced for its indifference. . . . If it expresses no political preferences it will be accused of siding with reaction and the status quo; if it supports progressive forces it will be condemned for intervention. In other words, we are damned if we do and damned if we don't.[2]

These predictions, now twenty-two years old, have, of course, been fulfilled. In 1970, partly as a result of these quandries, United States' official assistance to the developing countries reached its lowest point in nearly a decade. There is a general feeling that aid programs are not achieving their intended purpose. The answer of expert groups such as the Pearson Commission on International Development is essentially to pour in more money, the most often quoted target being 1 percent of GNP (roughly double the current U.S. amount).

But there is an understandable weariness about the reactions to such pleas. Both the public and the government are cautious about putting more money into programs which are widely considered to be inefficient and unsuccessful and which have contributed to a rising chorus of criticism of U.S. association with corrupt and repressive governments. In our view, then, no Administration can realistically expect to reverse the current downward trend in development assistance or the general feeling that trying to help the Third World may be futile until a more effective approach to development can be found.

In preceding chapters we have tried to identify some of the elements of a more effective approach. Before discussing how the United States might support this approach, we shall review the principal policies the United States and other rich countries have been pursuing in trying to help solve the problem of development and the lessons to be learned from our experience. These policies have been based on an attempt to identify a handful of key factors which were thought to represent the difference between developed and underdeveloped. What has happened is that "development experts" have identified key bottlenecks primarily in the light of Western experience and then devoted large amounts of resources to transferring Western solutions for the removal of these bottlenecks in the poor countries. Implicit in this approach is the premise that once a bottleneck is eliminated development would proceed apace. The developing countries would become stable, noncommunist mirrors of ourselves, and our relationships with them would be congenial and harmonious. Each proposed solution seemed so obviously right at the time and carried with it such a wave of optimism that each major policy adopted by the Western countries might almost be described as a fad. There have been four main fads in the past quarter century.

Four Development Fads

The first was the effort to transfer constitutions and democratic forms of government to the developing countries. We have already looked at this problem briefly in chapter 1. There we noted that in traditional societies the foundation of stability lay in the principle of reciprocity between rulers and ruled. The few with power had certain responsibilities towards the ruled, while the many who were ruled gave allegiance and certain kinds of tribute to the rulers. If the relationship ever began to break down (for example, because more tribute was demanded than could be afforded by the peasants), then the stability of the system began to break down. Indeed, in some societies the people were justified in overthrowing a ruler if he failed to carry out his responsibilities or if he violated the ethics of the society.

The coming of colonialism did much to break down this system. On the one hand, the ruling groups that the colonizing nations found it in their interests to support received the sanction of colonial power. And, on the other hand, these groups also discovered from the West new uses for their wealth and power. The common result was a strengthening of the exploitative and coercive aspects of the traditional relationships between ruler and ruled. The ruling groups could now demand more in the way of tribute and allegiance, while providing less in return. To give one example:

The system of land tenure in British India known as Zamindari was established in 1793 by the same Lord Cornwallis whom Washington defeated at Yorktown. His stated purpose was to assure adequate revenue for the East India Company, the private company which was Britain's agent in India at that time. The Zamindars were individuals of prominence in the various communities of India who agreed to deliver fixed sums to the British, in return for which they were given the right to collect rent from lands under their jurisdiction.

The Zamindars used the powers granted them under the "Permanent Settlement" to acquire vast holdings of land for themselves and to permit their agents to acquire land on a smaller scale in accordance with their rank. There was thus built up a hierarchy of exploiters of the peasantry supported by the might and majesty of the British Empire.

The system of Zamindari was not pure British invention. Rather, it was an adaptation of existing land tenure systems which the British set up in the course of consolidating their position on the sub-Continent. Although Zamindari was abolished after independence, many of the inequities of the system continued and are still a major obstacle to the advance of agriculture in India.

This is one illustration of how policies pursued throughout most of the colonial period conflicted with the last act of the colonial powers—the effort to leave behind workable democratic governments.

When independence came for the colonies, the West European nations and the United States seized upon the notion of democracy as practiced in the West as a way of at least adding some checks and balances to the system. Thus, nearly every developing country has had a constitution and a democratic superstructure grafted onto its colonial power system. It is perhaps hardly surprising, given the domination of these societies by elite groups, the inexperience of their new politicians, the levels of illiteracy and the ignorance of a national framework of the majority of their peoples, that this approach was not the panacea that was expected. In Europe and North America the democratic system, with all its imperfections, evolved over several centuries as ideas about the relationships among people and between people and their government gradually changed. In mechanically transferring our system to alien cultures and societies we introduced new political forms before ideas were evolved to give substance to the forms.

In a number of countries the democratic system has served merely to confirm and legitimize the precolonial power structure. Elections reflect the influence of the ruling groups rather than the wishes of the people. Parliaments have been established, but have little power. Rather, they tend to serve as safety valves, talking shops where grievances can be aired without much influence on prevailing problems. In these countries the democratic system lacks one of its crucial characteristics—choice.

In some countries, however, there has been an illusion of choice—much of Latin America and Asian countries such as Ceylon and the Philippines. There is more than one party, and governments have been changed peacefully in accordance with elections results. However, these parties represents a division among ruling groups rather than alternative choices for the nation at large. In addition, the competition between immature parties has often led to grossly unrealistic promises to the electorate, pledges that could not be redeemed by any party in power.

In both situations—no choice or an illusion of choice—there is a lack of effective participation by the people. And in both situations, the failure of the transplant to become a viable political system has led to a series of military coups, dictatorships, and one-party states.

The second bottleneck the West European and North American countries proposed to overcome was the shortage of trained manpower—Point IV, the original foreign aid program proposed by President Truman in 1948. On the one hand, primary education (literacy) was seen as an essential ingredient of the democratic system. On the other hand, vocational and university courses were established to make economic development occur. In each case, our institutions and curricula were transferred to the poor countries without much adaptation to the social and economic context into which they were being introduced.

Again, the results have tended to confound those who pinned their hopes on skill development programs as the key to development. Primary education, even where it contained elements relevant to agriculture, was seen as a passport out of stagnant rural areas. It has therefore contributed to rural-urban migration and the sucking of talented young people out of rural areas. At the same time, however, it has neither helped lay the foundations for viable democracy nor contributed to an expansion of entrepreneurship because the conditions of access for small farmers and small businessmen have not yet been created.

University and vocational education have also been less of a driving force for modernization than was originally hoped for. In chapter 7 we mentioned some of the deficiencies of existing education systems—the lack of relevance, rote memorization rather than problem solving, overemphasis on the formal school system, selecting the wrong kind of students for certain types of training programs.

There is one other difficulty. The supply of trained people has been multiplied many times over without creating the conditions in which their skills will be wanted and used. To illustrate: in traditional societies there is no need for agricultural extension agents because there is no sustained effort to increase agricultural productivity and farm income. However, simply training extension agents will not bring about rapid agricultural progress unless a country is also organizing a modern agricultural system and giving farmers access to it.

Hence, various types of formal education have not turned out to be the leading edge of development.

Almost coincident with the emphasis on training came the stress on industrialization as the key to development. Industrialization was equated with modernization and seen as the way to move from a society of subsistence farmers to the modern world. Planners in the developing countries and their North American and European advisers thought that the route to this transformation was to import the most advanced industrial processes. Economic policies such as overvalued exchange rates, low interest rates, tax holidays, and protection from foreign competition were designed to achieve this goal. In chapter 4, we saw how, in the context of the developing countries, this has resulted in unemployment, accelerated migration to the cities, the neglect of agriculture and intermediate industries, and the establishment of inefficient, capital-intensive enterprises.

The fourth policy of the North American and European countries stressed the importance of transfers of large amounts of money from the rich countries to the poor. The missing link in the development of the Third World was 1 percent of the gross national product of the industrialized nations. If only the latter group would be generous enough to provide this amount, as recommended by the Pearson Commission, then the necessary transformation of the poor countries would occur. When development experts acknowledged some failures in the development process, the cause was not the type of aid but the amount.

But in recent years, even the advocates of more aid are having difficulty in showing a relationship between aid (or high earnings from oil and mineral exports) and rapid economic growth, let alone the more complex problem of improving the lives of the world's poor. Much of the financial assistance from the rich countries has gone to sustain the predilections of the ruling elites in the developing countries, justified, as discussed in chapter 4, by misapplication of certain theorems of Western economics. Thus, government-to-government aid as well as that passing through the multilateral institutions has generally gone for capital-intensive projects or the import of capital-intensive machinery. Much aid has also been tied to the products of the donor country, thereby further reducing the ability of the poor countries to choose between technologies available in the different developed countries. The rich countries have, in these ways, reinforced and legitimized the desires of the poor countries for Western-style industrialization, with all the consequences that we have seen.

Democracy, training, modern factories, more money—these words sum up the major development policies of the Western democracies.

In the case of the United States, and to a lesser extent the other Western aid donors, the difficulties inherent in these simplistic solutions to development have been compounded by the general thesis of anticommunism which lay behind their policies towards the poor countries. As a result of this negative premise of our foreign policy, the United States has too often provided aid for countries with anticommunist governments, even though these governments were reluctant to make the changes necessary for broad-based development. In many poor countries, of course, the elites have professed anticommunism but have been unwilling or unable to create hope and opportunity for most of their people. In such cases, the United States has sometimes found itself propping up unpopular and unresponsive governments in the name of anticommunism or in support of previous commitments to status quo governments.

This identification of our land of opportunity with governments that deny opportunity is perhaps the major reason for the declining confidence of the people of the United States in foreign aid. It may also be the main cause of anti-Americanism in the Third World, an expression of disappointment at our seeming inability to help set in motion the needed processes of change.

Old Lessons, New Ideas

What lessons can we learn from these experiences?

There are perhaps two principal conclusions that can be drawn. The first is simply that development is a complex, historical process which does not lend itself to simplistic, quick solutions. Second, the role that the resources of the industrialized countries can play in development is rather limited, though our influence on ideas and attitudes in the developing countries is substantial. These two conclusions are perhaps self-evident, but their understanding is fundamental to determining what the rich nations can and should do with respect to the Third World.

Looking at the first of these two conclusions, we must try to understand the depth of change involved in setting off on the road to broad-based development. If the great mass of the people is to be brought into a modern society, the relationships among different groups of people, between rulers and ruled, and between people and their institutions must, in the long run, undergo far-reaching changes. This process has been underway for many generations in Europe and North America, and, of course, it never stops—it is a continuing process of innovation and adaptation to changing circumstance.

The history of the past fifty years has shown that in the countries that have experimented with both evolutionary and revolutionary forms of social organization, the use of these new forms to involve the mass of the people in development is a gradual and painstaking business. We cannot expect instant transformation in the developing countries.

However, those who want quick economic results sometimes oppose the kind of evolutionary policies proposed in this book because they seem to take too long. For example, it seems easier and much faster to call upon the large farmers to increase wheat production by 1/2 in just several years, as happened in India in the late 1960s, than to take the time to organize her 60 million farm families in cooperatives, local government, and other local institutions.

While it is true that change itself is gradual, the process of change can be introduced very quickly. What is needed most of all in the developing countries is the confidence that a better future is possible, a confidence implicit in the response of an Asian farmer in a modernizing situation, when asked why he was convinced a project would be completed, "We're doing it ourselves."

Despite these cautionary notes on the time perspective of development, we do not mean to suggest that little can be achieved in the foreseeable future. To the contrary, we believe the deceptively time-consuming process of organizing the people for development is nevertheless the most effective way of setting in motion the processes of evolutionary change. Throughout this book we have cited examples of the rapid progress which is possible when the people are involved in development. There can be rapid improvements in the lives of the world's poor in their nutritional and educational levels, standards of health and housing, infant and maternal mortality, and also their incomes and organizational affiliations. However, recognition of these improvements depends on more effective measures of poverty and what is happening to the poor as time passes. We now know, for example, that national statistics, such as GNP, tell us virtually nothing about changes in the income of the mass of small farmers. More accurate and more subtle measures of the true dimensions of poverty are needed.

The second conclusion to be drawn from the experiences of the past two decades concerns the role of the rich countries in assisting the developing countries. Only a handful of the countries escaped either the colonial experience of Asia and Africa or, in Latin America, the Spanish-Portuguese heritage of a rigid, stratified society, playing second fiddle to the United States.

These experiences have, of course, been extremely important in the creation of today's nation-states, in determining the power balances within these states, in forming the ideas and attitudes of the leaders of the poor countries, and also in reactions against us. In large measure, this direct role of the rich countries in the developing world has passed with the waning of colonialism and the granting of independence. In addition, the development of the post-Second World War superpower balances has imposed restraints on direct action by both sides.

However, the influence of Western ideas and advice has continued. It really is quite remarkable how many of the countries, for example, have tried to adopt constitutions and democratic forms of government as well as conspicuous modernization in the Western style. As we have seen, many of these ideas have been adopted unthinkingly as fads. There are, however, more fundamental ideas which have found universal appeal. Ideas about "life, liberty, and the pursuit of happiness," as well as ideas denying the fatalistic belief in traditional power relationships and the inevitability of poverty have been spread by education and other forms of communication. These ideas were, first of all, the driving force of the independence movements. These ideas are now the driving force of development.

Given this historical importance of outside ideas, there is no reason to expect that their influence will diminish as the developing countries strive to solve the dilemmas that face them. But there is ample reason to expect that many poor countries will experiment with ideas derived from Russian or Chinese experiences if they conclude that what they understand to be Western ideas, especially those relating to democracy, are failing to meet their critical needs. Another alternative, which we are trying to sketch out, is for the democratic, industrialized countries of North America and Europe to modify their ideas on development and to try to work with the developing countries, as partners rather than as superiors, as the countries struggle to find appropriate solutions to their own basic problems.

Turning from the realm of ideas to that of material assistance to the developing countries, we should try to put the significance of outside financial aid in perspective. There has been a sort of hidden assumption behind development assistance programs that if they did not exist there would be no progress in the developing countries, and world chaos would ensure. On the other hand, the poor countries' economies would grow rapidly if the rich countries were to provide 1 percent, now some $22 to 23 billion, of their gross national products.

In reality, external assistance will only contribute a small amount to development in the Third World as a whole, except in the unlikely event that assistance from the West is multiplied by several times. Development assistance transferred by the rich countries is only a small part of the poor countries' own savings or export earnings. In 1969, for example, the countries earned $49.5 billion in trade: they received only $6.4 billion (net) in development assistance from the numerous national and international aid agencies.[3] The impact of the assistance is greater than the rather small amount suggests, for two reasons. First, the distribution of export earnings among the developing countries is highly uneven. Some countries earn so much from oil and mineral exports that they do not need external financial help. On the other hand, the export earnings of some countries are so low that development assistance can raise the investment rate from low to high.

Second, some significant portion of the countries' export earnings is used to import consumption goods, such as food, whereas most development assistance is used for investment.

Granting these two points, the assumption for the Third World as a whole that progress in the countries depends heavily upon external help is unwarranted. Indeed, in the long run, the ideas of the West may be more significant than its wealth.

A Development Assistance Policy
for the Future

Given these caveats, we can ask the crucial question, "What should the U.S. policy and programs be with regard to development in the poor countries?"

We start with the premise that the United States will continue to have a variety of interests, described above, in the development of the poor countries. All of these should be strictly segregated from considerations of national security, since security so often conflicts with our other interests. In the few developing countries where the United States has a clearly defined national security interest, whatever help may be provided by us to support the incumbent government should be clearly separated from development assistance in both policy and administration. Such a separation will distinguish *ad hoc*, short-term goals from the more important long-term objectives of development policy.

With regard to development assistance, it is our view that the United States should focus its efforts on aiding broad-based development as described in this book. There are strong reasons for such a concentration. In the first place, this approach is likely to have the greatest effect on the real misery of life in the Third World, and so meet our humanitarian impulse toward the alleviation of social injustice and the extremes of poverty that are the lot of most of mankind. If the governments of the developing countries are willing, significant improvements can be made in even a few years.

And we must look to the future of the world. If present forms of development and development assistance continue, then the number of "marginal men" will increase rapidly. In the long run, it is hard to visualize stability in the world as this trend coincides with the revolution of rising expectations. There is, of course, no certainty that broad-based development will create peace. There is always the possibility that a few countries might try to use their newly-created wealth aggressively in the manner of Japan earlier in this century. Nevertheless, in our view, the human dignity and basic opportunities inherent in broad-based development are much more likely than present approaches to create the preconditions for a better, more stable world.

"Insofar as there is a relationship between industrialization and the emergence of democracy, it is that in the 19th century political freedom was considered a means to bring about economic advance. Democracy was then considered the most 'progressive' form of government, not only from the moral point of view but also because it was believed to be the most effective system for promoting material welfare."[4]

It is precisely this integration of economic growth, participation, and political freedom which is missing in the developing world today. Those who hope their countries can evolve in the direction of a free society, and they include numerous presidents and prime ministers of the past two decades, have lacked a strategy of modernization that combines all three. Since economic growth requires the application of specialized branches of knowledge, development has been treated as a bundle of technical subjects and made the responsibility of "experts." Further, there has been a tendency, often supported by North American and European advisers, to separate development from politics. Yet, development ought to be far and away the most important subject of politics throughout the Third World.

The economic policies of the countries and the aid agencies, carried out in the context of a dual society, have limited participation in economic development to a few, as discussed earlier. And welfare has been substituted for genuine participation.

Applying what we have described throughout this book as modernizing policies would permit a recombination of participation and economic growth. This is the essential first step in "the evolution of a different art of living and working together." Gradually the basic attitudes which guide the relationship among people can be changed in the direction of opportunity and dignity for all. If this evolutionary process is set in motion by national leaders who want their countries to become modern, free societies, then it may again be possible to combine participation and economic growth with political freedom, as in the late eighteenth and nineteenth centuries.

This is not to imply that the combination will be achieved easily. A nondemocratic country such as Taiwan has achieved a high level of economic growth and participation. As we have noted previously, the performance of Korea and Egypt, though mixed, is well above the Third World average. None of these countries, however, has yet tackled effectively the problem of combining economic growth and participation with political freedom.

How this combination can be brought about so that people will be able to influence the national political system is certain to be difficult. However, history tells us that there is little chance of expanding the realm of political freedom unless the process of increasing participation has already been set in motion. The success of the modernizing societies examined in this book has lain in their ability to start from where their people are, to create organizations and technologies that give the majority of their people more control over their destinies, and to do this within the boundaries of their own culture and tradition. These countries have not sought to impose on their people ready-made systems imported from alien societies, an approach which elsewhere has created benefits for a few and alienation and poverty for the many. Thus we conclude that hope for a better world and whatever prospect there is for democracy begins with modernizing policies.

How can the United States encourage such policies and what resources should be provided?

We believe the United States should take the initiative in the search for better ideas about getting development to the people. Our country should explain much more explicitly than we have in the past the criteria under which we are prepared to give development assistance, namely, to support modernizing policies which will gradually bridge the gap between rulers and ruled in a dual society. The world knows very well what we are against and has observed the pitfalls of a foreign policy based too much on a negative premise. Anticommunism is not a way of getting development to the people. But the world knows much too little about what we support.

Hopefully, the United States has learned from harsh experience the limitations of government by benevolence. Even the negative premise of anticommunism in our foreign policy is not, in the long run, served by supporting dual society governments that are reluctant to erode the ancient inhibitions that obstruct the adventurous.

The United States cannot, of course, act alone. The problem of development is of grave concern to all of the Western countries. It is also of grave concern to those in the developing countries who are trying to build a more humane social order.

But neither the United States, nor the rich democracies in concert, can presume to impose their will on the developing countries, even in the form of "expert advisers." The basic decisions about the future patterns of these societies, their organization, how they combine traditional and modern values, will increasingly be made in the developing countries themselves.

The period of the mechanical transfer of North American and European techniques and solutions is almost certainly coming to an end. It is true that many of the ideas which originated in our part of the world still retain great appeal in the countries. But the countries cannot use them effectively without some considerable process of adaptation to their own cultures, a process which only they can carry out.

We should also apply another lesson from the past two decades' experience which by now is self-evident; success begins with a country's willingness to modernize. If that willingness is lacking, help from the United States and other rich democracies, on any scale, is not an adequate substitute.

Hence, in the future we should be more selective in responding to requests for assistance. When governments are willing to institute modernizing policies, then we can help (if our help is requested) with some confidence that a more humane society will gradually evolve. Where development is concentrated among the few we should not feel constrained to help, even in the name of anticommunism. Assuming governments decide modernizing policies are worth pursuing, what changes would be needed in existing development programs? There are four major ones.

The first and most important change should be a shift away from "technical" and simplistic solutions—the more trained manpower, more factories, more money approach of the past two decades.

Instead, the planning of development programs should emphasize regional and especially local institutions and systems through which the people would be able to do the following:

1. Gain access to the economic and social system of their country
2. Learn how to use modern technology in their individual occupations and lives
3. Work in groups, such as their local government or their farmers' organization, to solve the problems of their local communities
4. Be linked to higher levels of the economy and the society

Money, machines, trained manpower, and other aspects of technical solutions, though obviously necessary for development, are secondary requirements.

With the second major change, the planning of development programs would be based on the assumption that the poor are both willing and able to pay the cost of their own improvement. Keeping the poor on disguised dole (such as extending agricultural credit without expectation of repayment) is not the way to increase the number of investors and the level of investment. In the beginning, when incomes are low and virtually static, savings will also be low. This is why governments and the development assistance agencies need to prime the pump in order to get started. But as incomes begin to rise, a substantial portion of the increase can be channeled into savings and investment. Financial and economic discipline is one of the characteristics of modernizing states.

The third major change: Much of the investment would be smaller in scale and at a simpler level of technology. Paved highways, high voltage transmission lines, and modern factories in the big cities will still be needed. But a higher proportion of a country's total resources should be used for organizing market towns; farm-to-market roads; small farm, labor-intensive agriculture; small-scale land improvement projects; small and "tiny" business; local consumer goods industries; and so forth.

The fourth change relates to the type of economic analysis used in planning development programs. Economists are presently working almost entirely with statistics which represent national totals, such as GNP, or national averages, such as per capita GNP. A number of topics need to be added to the conventional economic analysis of which the most important are: job creation, income distribution, the relative costs of capital and labor, and the influence of these on the pattern of savings and investment by small producers. In addition, economists should analyze development from the bottom up as well as from the top down. For example, there are now a number of excellent studies of overall agricultural and industrial development in Taiwan. There is barely a handful of studies on development from the point of view of individual Taiwanese farmers or small businessmen, or the township farmer cooperative, or industrial expansion in an individual market town, or the development of a local consumer goods industry. Yet these are the problems which interest individuals and local communities.[5]

In general, these are the major policy changes involved in introducing modernizing policies. The issues involved have been discussed in preceding chapters.

These changes would be needed in the development policies of both the poor countries and the development assistance agencies. What we are proposing is that the United States and other rich democracies should concentrate their development assistance in support of countries willing to sponsor modernizing policies.

Clearly, we cannot insist that the developing countries involve their people in development. Each government must set its own development policy. But just as we cannot impose our will on them, neither should we feel bound to accept whatever decisions the countries make. We are not obliged to support the development effort of every country in the Third World. Taxpayers have a right to expect our government not to invest in policies that do not get development to the people. Taxpayers are entitled to question why the United States, for example, should support the type of nonviable farmer cooperatives described in chapter 5.

Assuming developing countries set about increasing participation, and assuming outside assistance is both needed and wanted, how much should the United States try to help? Should we, for example, try to reach the target set by the Pearson Commission of 1 percent of GNP by 1975.[6] This would require appropriations several times higher than the Congress has been willing to approve in recent years. This lukewarm Congressional support for "foreign aid" is, of course, a reflection of a general lack of appreciation and agreement on the role the United States can play in development.

In our view, it is not possible to calculate what might be called "requirements for development assistance" from rich countries until we have had much more experience with the investment costs of modernizing policies. In addition, on the other side of the ledger there is no agreed way of determining how much rich countries "ought" to provide.

In any case, the crucial starting point is ideas, not the amount of money. While the kind of programs we are proposing could be introduced quickly, participation will build up gradually. Resources can be made available as success is demonstrated, but the United States and other countries will judge the amount of development assistance they can provide in the context of domestic needs. The important point would be the increased willingness of the rich nations to help those governments that are really trying to solve the fundamental human problems of development.

A Global Opportunity

We are fortunate to live in that period of history when the marginal people are persuaded that poverty is no longer inevitable and their role as nonpersons no longer tolerable. Enduring governments will be those that possess the will to set into motion the "evolution of a different art of living and working together."

Similarly, the long-run role of the United States in development will depend on our ability to help the poor countries create institutions and processes which are the means of evolutionary change. It is when people lose faith in peaceful change that they turn to revolutionary doctrine as an all-encompassing panacea for discontent.

Thus far, United States' assistance has not succeeded in getting at the heart of the human problems of development because we have relied too much on our riches and our military might. We have tied ourselves too closely to ruling groups that use United States support to bolster government by benevolence. We have tried too much to export our political forms to other countries.

In order to avoid the mistakes of the past and to carry out the policies proposed herein, we need to distinguish between the process of modernization and the form of the political superstructure. The United States can and should take a strong position in support of modernizing ideas and policies. We should curtail or terminate assistance to governments that continue to exclude the marginal masses from development. But we cannot insist that the developing countries try to copy our particular political forms. The problems which beset us at home are a reminder of the imperfections of our own system. The need for gentler and wiser government is not limited to developing countries. It is universal.

Notes

Notes

Chapter 1
Development Reconsidered

1. "Discourses on Davila," *Works*, Vol. 6 (Boston: Little, Brown, 1851), pp. 239-40.

2. B.S. Minhas, *Rural Poverty, Land Redistribution, and Development Strategy*, mimeo (Washington, D.C.: World Bank, 1970), p. 9.

3. International Labor Organization, *Towards Full Employment; A Programme for Colombia* (Geneva: ILO, 1970), p. 14. This study was prepared by an inter-agency team organized by the ILO.

4. David Turnham and Ingelies Jaeger, *The Employment Problem in Less Developed Countries—A Review of the Evidence* (Paris: Organization for Economic Cooperation and Development (OECD), 1970), pp. 58-59.

5. Doreen Warriner, *Land Reform in Theory and Practice* (London: Oxford University Press, 1969), p. 63.

6. Quoted in Vasily Kliuchevsky, *Peter the Great*, Archibald translation (New York: St. Martin's Press, 1958), p. 192.

7. Winston S. Churchill, *History of the English-Speaking Peoples*, Bantam edition (New York: 1963), 3:x.

8. This phrase is borrowed from the American anthropologist, Oscar Lewis, who argues that what the poor want is a "sense of belonging, of power and of leadership." There are a number of similarities between Professor Lewis' "culture of poverty" and our concept of the "marginal" masses. See *La Vida* (New York: Random House, 1965), introduction, pp. xlii-lii.

9. Kusum Nair, *Blossoms in the Dust* (New York: Frederick A. Praeger, 1962), p. 93.

10. Quoted in William McCord, *The Springtime of Freedom* (New York: Oxford University Press, 1964), p. 91.

11. M. George Zaninovich, *The Development of Socialist Yugoslavia* (Baltimore: Johns Hopkins Press, 1968), p. 119-21.

12. William and Charlotte Wiser, *Behind Mud Walls* (Berkeley: University of California Press, 1965), p. 120.

13. Quoted in Oscar Lewis, *The Children of Sanchez* (New York: Random House, 1961), p. 424.

14. The original reads, "None of the ancient inhibitions obstructed the adventurous," Churchill, *History*, 4:299.

15. John Stuart Mill, *On Liberty*.

16. *Democracy in America*, Phillips Bradley edition (New York: Alfred A. Knopf, Inc., 1951), p. 61.

17. Samuel P. Huntington, "Political Development and Political Decay," *World Politics* 17, no. 3 (April 1965): 415.

Chapter 2
Organizing People

1. Robert L. Heilbroner, "Counterrevolutionary America," *Commentary* 43, no. 4 (April 1967):32.

2. Edmund Burke, *Reflections on the Revolution in France* (New Rochelle, N.Y.: Arlington House, 1966), p. 33.

3. S.H. Frankel, quoted in Guy Hunter, *Modernizing Peasant Societies* (London: Oxford University Press, 1969), p. 139.

4. J.A.R. Marriott, *The Mechanisms of the Modern State* (Oxford: The Clarendon Press, 1937), 2:376.

5. Peter de Sautoy, *The Organization of a Community Development Program* (London: Oxford University Press, 1962), p. 85. This is a useful handbook on principles and operational methods of Community Development as it has been applied in the rural areas of the developing countries.

6. Some of the weaknesses of Traditional Community Development programs are discussed in ILO's *Towards Full Employment*, pp. 322-30; also Warriner, *Land Reform*, pp. 63 and 197-98.

7. In Western Europe, North America, and Japan, the ratio of agricultural extension workers varies from 1:700 to 1000. The ratio for VLW's in India would have been 1:300 if India had ever succeeded in reaching her initial goal of one per village.

8. John P. Lewis, *Quiet Crisis in India*, Doubleday Anchor edition (Garden City, N.Y.: Doubleday and Co., Inc., 1964), p. 177.

9. Min-hsioh-Kwoh, *Farmers' Associations and Their Contributions Toward Agricultural and Rural Development in Taiwan* (Bangkok: FAO Regional Office for Asia, 1964), p. 10.

10. Based on data in Martin M.E. Yang, *Socio-Economic Results of Land Reform in Taiwan* (Honolulu: East-West Center Press, 1970), p. 391.

11. Ibid., pp. 447-48.

12. S.C. Hsieh, "Agricultural Planning in Taiwan," reprinted in *Development Digest* 3, no. 3 (Washington, D.C.: United States Agency for International Development (AID), October 1965): 103-4.

Chapter 3
Organizing a National Economy

1. This chapter is based on regional planning theory. The first efforts to explain the relationship between economic activities and the organization of space was undertaken by Johann Heinrich von Thünen, *Isolated State*, originally published in Rostock, 1826 (English translation by Carla M. Wartenberg, Peter Hall, Oxford, 1966). Since then the subject has been developed extensively in

several different academic disciplines: economic geography, market theory, industrial location theory, and, most recently, in sociology by Professor Frank Young of Cornell University. The American who has done most to apply the theory to the developing countries is Professor E.A.J. Johnson, of the Johns Hopkins University School for Advanced International Studies, Washington, D.C. This chapter draws considerably on two of Professor Johnson's books, *Market Towns and Spatial Development in India* (New Delhi: National Council of Applied Economic Research, 1965), and *The Organization of Space in Developing Countries* (Cambridge, Mass.: Harvard University Press, 1970). The first book was published in India and, unfortunately, has never been distributed in Europe or North America. Somewhat unexpectedly, perhaps, regional planning is widespread in the socialist countries, but elsewhere in the Third World it is uncommon. See Albert Waterston, *Development Planning*, Johns Hopkins Press, Baltimore, Maryland, 1965, chapter 16.

2. United National Economic Commission for Latin America (ECLA), *Economic Survey of Latin America*, 1968 (New York: United Nations, 1970), table 22, p. 25.

3. John P. Lewis, *Quiet Crisis*, p. 193.

4. Ibid., p. 191.

5. Commission on International Development, *Partners in Development* (New York: Frederick A. Praeger, 1969), p. 61. The Commission was appointed by World Bank President Robert McNamara to "study the consequences of twenty years of development assistance, assess the results, clarify the errors and propose the policies which will work better in the future." It is sometimes referred to as the Pearson Report, after the Commission's Chairman, former Canadian Prime Minister, Lester B. Pearson.

6. An excellent discussion of economic and uneconomic systems of rural electrification is contained in E.A.J. Johnson, *The Organization of Space in Developing Countries* (Cambridge, Mass.: Harvard University Press, 1970), pp. 264-74.

7. *Population Census of India*, 1961 (New Delhi: The Manager of Publications, 1963).

8. Abraham Kaplan, quoted in *Regional Economic Planning, Techniques of Analysis for Less Developed Areas,* eds. Walter Isard and John H. Cumberland (Paris: Organization for European Economic Cooperation, 1961), p. 142.

9. Puerto Rico Planning Board, *Four Year Economic and Social Development Plan of Puerto Rico* (San Juan, 1968), p. 61.

10. This phrase is actually part of the title of a book on the organization of space for rural development: A.T. Mosher, *Creating a Progressive Rural Structure to Serve a Modern Agriculture* (New York: Agricultural Development Council, 1969).

11. Dr. Mosher is one of the very few students of rural development who has attempted to analyze the requirement for farm-to-market roads. See *Creating a*

Progressive Rural Structure, pp. 16-21. The model he uses in discussing the problem works out to a minimum of 2 miles of roads per square mile of cultivated land.

12. Wilfred Owen, *Distance and Development* (Washington, D.C.: The Brookings Institution, 1968), p. 53.

13. E.A.J. Johnson, *Market Towns and Spatial Development in India* (New Delhi: National Council of Applied Economic Research, 1965), pp. 131-37.

14. Johnson, *Organization of Space*, pp. 217-22; Mosher, *Creating a Progressive Rural Structure*, chapter 5.

15. Two recent research studies which tend to support this statement are: Stanford Research Institute, School of Planning and Architecture (New Delhi), Small Industry Extension Training Institute, *Costs of Urban Infrastructure for Industry as Related to City Size in Developing Countries: India Case Study*, prepared under contract for the U.S. Agency for International Development, 1968; and S.K. Bhatia, *The Current Cost of Urbanization in Pakistan* (Washington, D.C.: The World Bank, 1970).

16. For an excellent discussion of housing problems in the developing countries, see: Charles Abrams, *Man's Struggle for Shelter* (Cambridge, Mass.: M.I.T. Press, 1964).

Chapter 4
Efficient Use of the Exploding Labor Force

1. Robert McNamara, President, World Bank, "Address to the Board of Governors, World Bank Group," Copenhagen, Sept. 21, 1970.

2. David A. Morse, "Special Dimensions of the Employment Problem in Developing Countries" (Keynote Paper at Cambridge Conference on Development, Cambridge University, Sept. 1970).

3. J.N. Ypsilantis, "World and Regional Estimates and Projections of the Labor Force" (Paper submitted by the ILO to the Inter-regional Seminar on Long-Term Economic Projections for the World Economy, Elsinore, Denmark, 1966). See also United Nations Economic and Social Council (ECOSOC), "Creation of Job Opportunities and Training of Cadres in Countries Undergoing Rapid Modernization" (E/CN, 5/422, 9 November 1967), p. 9.

4. G. Tobias, "Human Resources Utilization and Development in the Seventies," New Delhi, The Ford Foundation, 1970 (mimeo), pp. 3-4.

5. Eric Thorbecke, "Unemployment and Underemployment in the Developing World" in Barbara Ward (ed.) *The Widening Gap: Development in the 1970s* (New York: Columbia University Press, 1971), pp. 116-118.

6. ILO, *Towards Full Employment*, p. 13.

7. The first figures are quoted in Robert D'A. Shaw, *Jobs and Agricultural Development* (Washington, D.C.: Overseas Development Council, 1970), p. 67; the second from the *Washington Post*, September 1, 1970.

8. David Turnham and Ingelies Jaeger, *The Employment Problem in Less Developed Countries—A Review of the Evidence* (Paris: Organization for Economic Cooperation and Development, 1971), table 2, pp. 48-49.

9. Tobias, *Human Resources*.

10. Solon Barraclough, "Employment Problems Affecting Latin American Agricultural Development," *Monthly Bulletin of Agricultural Economics and Statistics* 18, nos. 7/8 (July/August 1969): 1. This increase in the size of the farm labor force is occurring even though agricultural employment has fallen from 54 percent of the total work force in 1950 to an estimated 45 percent in 1968 and is expected to drop to about 40 percent by 1980.

11. Hiromitsu Kaneda, *Economic Implications of the Green Revolution and the Strategy of Agricultural Development in West Pakistan*, Research Report no. 78 (Karachi: Institute of Development Economics, 1969), p. 7.

12. S.V. Sethuraman, "Prospect for Increasing Employment in Indian Manufacturing," in Ronald Ridker and Harold Lubell (Eds.), *Employment and Unemployment Problems of the Near East and South Asia* (New Delhi: Vikas Publications, 1971), table I, 2:624.

13. For an excellent technical discussion of the issues discussed in this chapter, see Keith Marsden, "Towards a Synthesis of Economic Growth and Social Justice," *International Labour Review* 100, no. 5 (November, 1969): 389-418.

14. B.H. Pollitt, "Employment Plans, Performance, and Future Prospects in Cuba," Ronald Robinson, and Peter Johnston, (eds.), "Prospects for Employment Opportunities in the Nineteen Seventies" (London: HMSO, 1971), p. 60.

15. This is the report, *Towards Full Employment*, cited previously. The director of the ILO studies is the British economist, Dudley Seers.

16. ILO, *Towards Full Employment*, p. 49.

17. *Change and Development: Latin America's Great Task* (Washington, D.C.: Inter-American Development Bank, 1970).

18. Report of the Commission on International Development, *Partners in Development* (New York: Frederick A. Praeger, 1969), p. 58.

19. The price distortions in the Asian Green Revolution countries are discussed in Falcon, "The Green Revolution: Generations of Problems," (Paper presented to the Summer Meeting of the American Agricultural Economics Association, Columbia, Missouri, August, 1970), pp. 13-15; Kaneda, *Green Revolution*, pp. 28-31.

20. Statistics of this sort are a quick way of indicating the very small size of farms in the crowded countries. They are, however, somewhat misleading in that the potential income from a particular farm depends on a number of environmental factors in addition to farm size. For example, in tropical or semi-tropical areas where temperatures are mild throughout the year, if irrigation is possible a 2½ acre farm becomes, in effect, a 5 to 10 acre farm through multiple cropping— as in Japan and Taiwan. The effective size of the farm depends on the cropping pattern. In Taiwan and Japan two crops of rice plus a vegetable crop are common (in addition to a number of other variations). It is possible a 2½ acre farm

in many parts of monsoon, tropical Asia could yield as much income as 10 to 20 acres in light rainfall, nonirrigable areas in other parts of the world.

21. Bruce F. Johnston, "Agriculture and Economic Development: The Relevance of the Japanese Experience," *Food Research Institute Studies* 6, no. 3 (Stanford University, 1966): 288. This brilliant and relatively brief analysis of a Japanese-style agricultural revolution ought to be required reading for planners in both the developing countries and the aid agencies.

22. Peter Dorner and Don Kanel, "The Economic Case for Land Reform," *Spring Review on Land Reform* (Proceedings of a conference sponsored by the United States Agency for International Development, Washington, D.C., 1970), 11:22. Available from National Technical Information Service, Department of Commerce, Washington, D.C.

23. The most extensive studies on the economics of farm size have been carried on by the Land Tenure Center of the University of Wisconsin. See Lester Schmid, *Relation of Size of Farm to Productivity*, LTC, University of Wisconsin, 1969. See also Don Kanel, "Size of Farm and Economic Development," *Indian Journal of Agricultural Economics* 22 (April-June 1967): 26-64, also issued as Land Tenure Center Reprint, no. 31; Erven J. Long, "The Economic Basis of Land Reform in Underdeveloped Countries," *Land Economics* 37 (May 1961): 113-23; Dorner and Kanel, "Economic Case for Land Reform."

24. Folke Dovring, "Land Reform in Mexico," *Spring Review* 7:44-48 and 50-54.

25. Warriner, *Land Reform*, pp. 39, 400.

26. Johnston, p. 288.

27. Roger Lawrence, "Some Economic Aspects of Farm Mechanization in Pakistan," Study prepared for U.S.A.I.D., Washington, D.C., 1970, mimeo., pp. 15-17. "Chisel ploughing loosens the soil down to a depth of 14-16 inches, and can be accomplished only with tractor power. This ploughing breaks up the hard pan which lies 4 to 5 inches under the surface and which prevents rainfall from seeping into the soil beyond this depth." Deep ploughing increases the moisture retention qualities so much that yields, which are now among the lowest in the world, can be increased several times.

28. Asian Development Bank, *Asian Agricultural Survey* (Tokyo, 1968), p. 568; Shaw, *Jobs*, p. 34; and Kaneda, *Green Revolution*, p. 21.

29. One well-known American agricultural economist recently wrote about India: "Modern units of agricultural technology are often too large for the small farmer to incorporate them efficiently into his operation." Willard W. Cochrane, "Some Notes on Indian Food and Agricultural Policy," *Symposium on Development and Change in Traditional Agriculture*, Asian Studies Center (East Lansing, Michigan: Michigan State University, 1968), p. 27.

30. Warriner, *Land Reform*, p. 134.

31. See Warriner's *Land Reform* for a discussion of the efficiency of collective farms, pp. 64-73; also, Folke Dovring, "Land Reform in Yugoslavia," *Spring Review* 10:40-46.

32. Asian Productivity Organization (APO), *Report of the Expert Group Meeting on Agricultural Mechanization* (Tokyo, 1968): table 30, p. 50.

33. S.R. Bose and E.H. Clark, "Some Basic Considerations on Agricultural Mechanization in West Pakistan," *Pakistan Development Review* 9, no. 3 (Autumn 1969): 273-308. See also Kaneda, *Green Revolution*, pp. 42-47, for a discussion of agricultural mechanization, and Shaw, *Jobs*, pp. 31-40, 57-60.

34. Keith Marsden, "Economic Growth with Social Justice," *International Labor Review* 100, no. 5 (Nov. 1969): 410-11. Two studies still in process at the time of writing also provide convincing evidence of advantages of small-scale, labor-intensive industry, at least in the early stages of development. They are John E. Todd, "Size of Farm and Efficiency in Colombian Manufacturing," Williams College, Williamstown, Mass., and Albert Berry, "Relevance and Prospects for Small-Scale Industry in Colombia," Yale University Economic Growth Center, New Haven, Conn.

35. William W. Lockwood, *The Economic Development of Japan* (Princeton: Princeton University Press, 1954), p. 25.

36. Edward H. Smith, "The Diesel Engine Industry of Pakistan's Punjab: Implications for Development," Preliminary draft of a Ph.D. dissertation, Yale University, 1970.

37. Keith Marsden, "Progressive Technologies for Developing Countries," *International Labor Review* 101, no. 5 (May 1970): 483, fn. 4, and M.M. Mehta, *Employment Aspects of Industrialization with Special Reference to Asia and the Far East* (Bangkok: ILO, 1970), pp. 43-47.

38. Harry T. Oshima, "Labor-Force 'Explosion' and the Labor-Intensive Sector in Asian Growth," *Economic Development and Cultural Change* 19, no. 2 (January 1971): 171-78.

39. ILO, *Towards Full Employment*, pp. 148-49.

40. Commission on International Development, *Partners*, pp. 59-60.

41. Oshima, "Labor-Force 'Explosion,' " p. 178.

Chapter 5
A Policy for Developing Farmers

1. Johnston, "Agriculture: Relevance of Japan," p. 285.

2. Francine Frankel, "India's New Strategy of Agricultural Development: Political Cost of Agrarian Modernization," *Journal of Asian Studies* no. 4 (September 1969), :693-695.

3. Ibid., p. 706. The so-called "miracle seeds" are grown most efficiently on irrigated land because they require large quantities of water and carefully controlled water levels. The seeds are not grown much on rain-fed land because of the uncertainty of the water supply. In irrigation, as in other elements of a modern agricultural system, the larger farmers tend to have greater access. Many small farms are located on marginal, non-irrigable lands. For this reason, the

decision to initiate research on high-yielding seeds for irrigated areas was actually a political decision that favored the rich.

4. Shaw's *Jobs* discusses the mechanization question (chapter 4) and also contains an extensive bibliography of recent studies on the subject.

5. Frankel, "India's New Strategy," pp. 699-700.

6. United States Department of Agriculture, *Increasing World Food Output* (Washington, D.C., 1965), p. 115.

7. Oscar Lewis, *Five Families* (New York: Basic Books, 1959), pp. 9-10.

8. Roger D. Hansen, *The Politics of Mexican Development* (Baltimore: Johns Hopkins Press, 1971), pp. 81, 210.

9. Warriner, *Land Reform*, pp. 402-403.

10. United Nations Research Institute for Social Development (UNRISD), *Rural Institutions and Planned Change*, 2 (Geneva, 1970), p. 293.

11. Ibid., p. 291.

12. Warriner, *Land Reform*, p. 39.

13. UNRISD, *Rural Institutions*, 1:331.

14. Min-hsioh Kwoh, *Farmers' Associations . . . in Taiwan*, pp. 41-62.

15. The statistics in this paragraph are taken from, Mohindar Singh, *Cooperatives in Asia* (New York: Frederick A. Praeger, 1970), p. 52, the *FAO Production Yearbook* (Rome, 1969), and *Statistical Abstract of the Indian Union*, (Central Statistical Office, Delhi, 1970), published annually.

16. Reported in Warriner, *Land Reform*, p. 129.

17. Ibid., p. 80.

18. Y.T. Chang, "Food Problems in Taiwan," in *Food Problems in Asia and the Pacific* (Proceedings of a Seminar held at East-West Center, Honolulu, 1970), p. 254.

19. Folke Dovring, "Land Reform in Mexico," *Spring Review*, 7:51, Table 13.

20. Dr. Richard Newburg, an agricultural economist with the United States Agency for International Development.

21. So far as I know, the first person to suggest there might be what we are calling a Gresham's Law of Farm Size and System was Kusum Nair, the distinguished Indian author of *Blossoms in the Dust* and *The Lonely Furrow*.

22. Shaw, *Jobs*, pp. 24-25.

23. Nineteenth General Report of the Joint Commission on Rural Reconstruction, Taipei, Taiwan, 1968, p. 100.

24. The figures in both paragraphs are from Singh, *Cooperatives in Asia*, table 7, p 70

25. Ibid., p. 105; Guy Hunter, *The Administration of Agricultural Development* (London: Oxford University Press, 1970), p. 134. The same point is also discussed in the various UN case studies of farmer cooperatives, UNRISD, *Rural Institutions*, and Warriner, *Land Reform*.

26. Arthur Raper, and others, *Rural Development in Action* (Ithaca, N.Y.: Cornell University Press, 1970), pp. 65-72.

27. Academy for Rural Development, Comilla, Bangladesh, 9th Annual Report, "A New Rural Cooperative System for Comilla Thana [county] , 1968-69."

28. UNRISD, *Rural Institutions*, 2:41.

29. Ibid., p. 43.

30. Information provided by Dr. John Eklund, President, Agricultural Cooperative Development International (ACDI), Washington, D.C. ACDI is an organization of American farmers cooperatives which works in Uganda and other developing countries, usually on contract with the United States Agency for International Development.

31. Stephen Hymer in the foreward to Polly Hill's *Rural Capitalism in West Africa* (London: Cambridge University Press, 1970), p. xix.

32. Johnston, "Agriculture: Relevance of Japan," p. 283.

33. The taxes are based on data contained in S.K. Shen, "Land Taxation as Related to Land Reform Program in Taiwan," in Archibald M. Woodruff, James R. Brown, and Sein Lin (eds.), *Land Taxation, Land Tenure, and Land Reform in Developing Countries* (West Hartford, Connecticut: University of Hartford, 1966), p. 337.

34. T.H. Lee, "Strategies for Transferring Agricultural Surplus Under Different Agricultural Situations in Taiwan," mimeo., Taipei, 1971. Dr. Lee is Chief, Rural Economics Division, Joint Commission on Rural Construction, Taiwan.

35. Johnston, "Agriculture: Relevance of Japan," p. 281.

36. M.L. Dantwala, "Agriculture Taxation and Land Reform in India," in *Land Taxation*, pp. 273-299.

37. William Arthur Lewis, "Comment on Agriculture Taxation in a Developing Country," in Herman M. Southworth and Bruce F. Johnston (eds.), *Agricultural Development and Economic Growth* (Ithaca, N.Y.: Cornell University Press, 1967), p. 494.

38. Johnston, "Agriculture: Relevance of Japan," p. 287.

39. FAO, *The State of Food and Agriculture, 1970* (Rome: FAO, published annually, 1970), pp. 83-84. The FAO also cites West Malaysia and Indonesia as examples of the agricultural strategy described in the quotation. We have discussed Ceylon because it is the most successful of the three. See also P. Richards and E. Stoutjesdik, *Agriculture in Ceylon Until 1975* (Paris: Development Centre of the Organisation for Economic Co-operation and Development, 1970).

40. Johnston, "Agriculture: Relevance of Japan," p. 288.

Chapter 6
Industrializing the National Economy

1. Keith Marsden, "Progressive Technologies for Developing Countries," *International Labour Review*, vol. 101, no. 5 (May, 1970), :488.

2. Saburo Okita, "Choice of Techniques: Japan's Experience and its Impli-

cation," in *Economic Development with Special Reference to East Asia*, ed. Kenneth Berril (New York: St. Martin's Press, 1964), p. 382.

3. Cited in Marsden, "Progressive Technologies," p. 480.

4. Mehta, *Employment Aspects*, p. 66.

5. Cited in H.W. Singer, "International Policies and Their Effect on Employment," in Robinson and Johnson (eds.), *Prospects for Employment*, p. 200.

6. Mehta, *Employment Aspects*, p. 4.

7. Based on statistics printed in *Statistical Bulletin for Latin America*, published annually by the United Nations; and *Economic Survey of Latin America*, 1968, published annually by the UN Economic Commission for Latin America.

8. Prebisch, *Change and Development*, pp. 26-33.

9. Ibid., p. 29.

10. Lockwood, *Economic Development of Japan*, p. 198.

11. Mehta, *Employment Aspects*, p. 25.

12. Smith, "Diesel Engine Industry."

13. Cited in Eugene Staley and Richard Morse, *Modern Small Industry for Developing Countries* (New York: McGraw-Hill, 1965), p. 233.

14. Bruce F. Johnston and Peter Kilby, "Agricultural Strategy and Industrial Growth: A Report on Visits to Taiwan, India and West Pakistan," 1969, mimeo., p. 27. Similar problems of lack of access for small entrepreneurs in Colombia are discussed in ILO, *Towards Full Employment*, passim.

15. Smith, "Diesel Engine Industry."

16. Hiromitsu Kaneda and Frank C. Child, *Small-Scale, Agriculturally Related Industry in the Punjab*, Working Paper Series, number 11 (University of California at Davis, Cal., 1971), p. 2, fn. 2.

17. ILO, *The Development of Small Enterprises in Taiwan* (Geneva, 1967), table 4, p. 37.

18. This description is culled from Staley and Morse, *Modern Small Industry*, pp. 391-397.

19. S. Watanabe, "Entrepreneurship in Small Enterprises in Japanese Manufacturing," *International Labour Review*, 102, no. 6 (December, 1970), :531-576.

20. Johnson, *Spatial Development in India*, p. 90.

21. Ibid., p. 80-93.

22. ILO, *Towards Full Employment*, p. 147.

23. Douglas S. Paauw, "Strategies for the Transition from Economic Colonialism to Sustained Modern Growth," condensed and reprinted in *Development Digest*, 8, no. 4 (October 1970), :117.

24. ILO, *Small Enterprises in Taiwan*, table 7, p. 38.

25. Lockwood, *Economic Development of Japan*, pp. 488-491.

Chapter 7
The Significance of Non-Formal Education

1. Kusum Nair, *Blossoms in the Dust*, p. 149.

2. Ibid., 151.

3. Edward Smith, "Diesel Engine Industry."

4. Ibid.

5. Yang, *Land Reform in Taiwan* , 525.

6. UNRISD, *Rural Institutions*, 6:30.

7. Yang, *Land Reform in Taiwan*, p. 468.

8. Jon Moris, "Farmer Training as a Strategy of Rural Development," in *Education, Employment and Rural Development*, James E. Sheffield ed. (Nairobi, Kenya: East African Publishing House, 1967), p. 332.

9. William Mangin, "Latin American Squatter Settlements: A Problem and a Solution," reprinted and condensed in *Development Digest* 6, no. 3 (July 1968), 41-49.

10. Frederick H. Harbison, and George Seltzer, "National Training Schemes" (Paper prepared for a seminar conducted by the Southeast Asia Development Advisory Group, May 1971), pp. 2-8.

11. The statistics underlying this paragraph are from *The Statesman's Yearbook*, published annually since 1864 by St. Martin's Press, London.

Chapter 8
Population and Exports as Evidence

1. Frank Lorimer, "Issues of Population Policy," in *The Population Dilemma*, 2nd Edition, Philip M. Hauser ed. (Englewood Cliffs, N.J.: Prentice-Hall, 1969), p. 179. Published for the American Assembly.

2. See A.M. Carr-Saunders, *World Population*, for a detailed exposition of the classical population curve and an analysis of population trends in Western Europe. Carr-Saunders was the first modern demographer.

3. Yang, *Land Reform in Taiwan*, p. 446.

4. Professor Bruce F. Johnston, has also observed this relationship between modernizing policies and the birth rate: "Not the least of the advantages of a strategy of agricultural development that involves the bulk of the farm population is the likelihood . . . that this will provide a relatively propitious environment for fostering the changes necessary to the spread of family planning." "Agriculture: Relevance of Japan," p. 301.

5. The argument in this section is based on: Barend de Vries, *Export Experiences of Developing Countries*, World Bank Staff Occasional Papers, No. 3 (Washington, D.C.: World Bank, Distributed by The Johns Hopkins Press, Baltimore, 1967); Ian M.D. Little, Tibor Scitovsky, and Maurice Scott, *Industry and Trade in Some Developing Countries* (London: Oxford University Press, 1970); and Douglas S. Paauw and John C.H. Fei, *The Transition in Open Dualistic Economies* (Washington, D.C.: National Planning Association, 1970).

Chapter 9
The United States and the
Developing Countries

1. Address to the Board of Governors, World Bank Group, Copenhagen, September 21, 1970.

2. *New York Times*, 15 October 1950.

3. *Trade and Development: Trade Performance and Prospects of Developing Countries* (Washington, D.C.: AID 1971), p. 4.

4. Kissinger, Henry, *The Necessity for Choice* (New York: Harper and Row, 1960), p. 291.

5. One economist, Polly Hill, has written an eloquent plea for what she calls "indigenous economics." In her own research she concentrates on "producers rather than on production." See her, *Rural Capitalism in West Africa* (London: Cambridge University Press, 1970), especially the introduction by Professor Hymer of Yale University and chapter 1, "A Plea for Indigenous Economics: The West African Example."

6. Commission on International Development, *Partners*, chapter 7. The Commission recommended that what is commonly called "foreign aid" that is, development assistance provided by governments, should be .7 of 1 percent of GNP. The remainder of the 1 percent consists of private investment and commercial transactions of several kinds, such as private bank purchases of World Bank bonds.

Bibliography

Bibliography

(Authors' Note: We have omitted from this bibliography the standard texts in political science, economic development, agricultural economics, sociology and anthropology which are well known to students of development and commonly available in libraries throughout the world. Rather, the bibliography is limited to a small number of references that are related to the arguments presented in this book.)

Arendt, Hannah. *On Revolution*. New York: The Viking Press, 1963.

Commission on International Development. *Partners in Development*. New York: Frederick A. Praeger, 1969.

de Jesus, Carolina Maria. *Child of the Dark*. New York: Dutton, 1962.

Fanon, Franz. *The Wretched of the Earth*. London: MacGibbon and Kee, 1965.

Hansen, Roger D. *The Politics of Mexican Development*. Baltimore: Johns Hopkins Press, 1971.

Heilbroner, Robert L. "Counterrevolutionary America," *Commentary* 43, No. 4 (April 1967), 31-38.

Hill, Polly. *Rural Capitalism in West Africa*. London: Cambridge University Press, 1970.

Hunter, Guy. *Modernizing Peasant Societies*. London: Oxford University Press, 1969.

Huntington, Samuel P. *Political Order in Changing Societies*. New Haven: Yale University Press, 1968.

International Labor Organization (ILO). *Towards Full Employment: A Programme for Colombia*. Geneva, 1970.

_____ . *Matching Employment Opportunities and Expectations: A Programme of Action for Ceylon*. Geneva, 1971.

Jacoby, Neil N. *United States Aid to Taiwan: A Study of Foreign Aid*. New York: Frederick A. Praeger, 1967.

Johnson, E.A.J. *Market Towns and Spatial Development in India*. New Delhi: National Council of Applied Economic Research, 1965.

Johnson, E.A.J. *Organization of Space in Developing Countries*. Cambridge, Mass.: Harvard University Press, 1970.

Johnston, Bruce F. "Agriculture and Economic Development: The Relevance of the Japanese Experience," *Food Research Institute Studies*, 6 no. 3 (Stanford University, 1966), pp. 251-312.

Kaneda, Hiromitsu. "Economic Implications of the Green Revolution and the Strategy of Agricultural Development in West Pakistan." Karachi, Institute of Development Economics, Research Report No. 78, 1969.

Lewis, John P. *Quiet Crisis in India*. Washington, D.C.: Brookings Institution, 1962.

179

Lewis, Oscar. *La Vida*. New York: Random House, 1965.

_____. *Children of Sanchez*. New York: Random House, 1961.

_____. *Pedro Martinez: A Mexican and His Family*. New York: Random House, 1964.

Lewis, Sir William Arthur. *The Theory of Economic Growth*. Homewood, Ill.: Richard D. Irwin, 1955.

Lockwood, William W. *The Economic Development of Japan*. Princeton, N.J.: Princeton University Press, 1954.

Marsden, Keith. "Towards A Synthesis of Economic Growth and Social Justice," *International Labour Review*, 100, no. 5 (November 1969): 389-418.

_____. "Progressive Technologies for Developing Countries," *International Labour Review*, 101, no. 5 (May 1970): 475-502.

McNamara, Robert. "Address to the Board of Governors, World Bank Group." Sept. 27, 1971. Washington, D.C.

Mehta, M.M. *Employment Aspects of Industrialization with Special Reference to Asia and the Far East*. Bangkok, ILO, 1970.

Mosher, Arthur T. *Creating a Progressive Rural Structure*. New York, Agricultural Development Council, 1969.

_____. *Getting Agriculture Moving*. New York. Agricultural Development Council, 1966.

Myrdal, Gunnar. *Asian Drama*. New York: Twentieth Century Fund, 1968.

Nair, Kusum. *Blossoms in the Dust*. New York, Frederick A. Praeger, 1962.

_____. *The Lonely Furrow*. Ann Arbor, Michigan: University of Michigan Press, 1969.

Owen, Wilfred. *Distance and Development*. Washington, D.C.: The Brookings Institution, 1968.

Prebisch, Raul. *Change and Development: Latin America's Great Task*. Washington, D.C., Inter-American Development Bank, 1970.

Robinson, Ronald and Johnston, Peter (Eds.). *Prospects for Employment Opportunities in the Nineteen Seventies*. Cambridge Conference on Development, Cambridge University, September, 1970. London: HMSO, 1971.

Task Force on International Development: *U.S. Foreign Assistance in the 1970s: A New Approach*, Report to the President of the United States. Washington, D.C.: Government Printing Office, March 4, 1970.

Turnham, David and Jaeger, I. *The Employment Problem in Less Developed Countries—A Review of the Evidence*. Paris: Organization for Economic Co-operation and Development (OECD), 1970.

Ward, Barbara (ed). *The Widening Gap*, A report on the Columbia Conference on International Economic Development, Williamsburg, Virginia, February 15-21, 1970. New York: Columbia University Press, 1971.

Warriner, Doreen. *Land Reform in Theory and Practice*. London: Oxford University Press, 1969.

Weitz, Raanan. *From Peasant to Farmer*. New York and London: Columbia University Press, 1971.

Wiser, Charlotte V. and William H. *Behind Mud Walls, 1930-1960*. Berkeley: University of California Press, 1965.

Yang, Martin M.E. *Socio-Economic Results of Land Reform in Taiwan*. Honolulu: East-West Center Press, 1970.

Index

About the Authors

Edgar Owens has worked for the United States Agency for International Development since 1960 and has served in Pakistan, Bangladesh, South Vietnam and Thailand.

He earned an A.B. degree in Political Science from Dickinson College in 1948, and did graduate study at Syracuse University, Syracuse, N.Y., and at the London School of Economics and Political Science. He was Federal Executive Fellow of the Brookings Institution in Washington, D.C. from 1965-66.

His publications include *Farmer Cooperatives in Developing Countries*, published by the Advisory Committee on Overseas Cooperative Development, Washington, D.C., 1971, and several articles on rural development.

Robert Shaw has been a Research Fellow of the Overseas Development Council, Washington, D.C., and is joining the World Bank in March 1972. He was administrator of the British Volunteer Program in Tanzania from 1966-68.

His education includes both B.A. and M.A. degrees in Social Anthropology from Cambridge University, completed in 1965. He received an M.P.A. degree from Woodrow Wilson School, Princeton University, in 1972.

His published works include *Jobs and Agricultural Development*, Overseas Development Council Monograph No. 3, 1970; *Rethinking Economic Development*, Foreign Policy Association, Headline Series, No. 208, 1971; as well as numerous articles on rural development and employment.